DEPARTURES

DEPARTURES

REFLECTIONS IN POETRY

EDITED BY JAMES BARRY

BREBEUF COLLEGE SCHOOL

Nelson Canada

© Nelson Canada,
A Divison of Thomson Canada Limited, 1991
1120 Birchmount Road
Scarborough, Ontario
M1K 5G4

ISBN 0-17-603717-9
Teacher's Guide 0-17-603718-7

To Mary- Louise

Project Manager: Lana Kong
Project Editor: David Friend
Art Director: Lorraine Tuson
Designer: Gail McGowan
Cover and Interior Illustration: Stéphan Daigle
Cover Illustration: Stéphan Daigle
Typesetting: Nelson Canada

Printed and bound in Canada

14 15 16 17 18 TCP 08 07 06 05 04

Canadian Cataloguing in Publication Data

Main entry under title:

Departures : reflections in poetry

ISBN 0-17-603717-9

1.   Canadian poetry (English).* 2. American poetry.
3.   English poetry. I. Barry, James, date.

PN6101.D46 1990   821.008   C90-094151-0

We would like to thank the following people who contributed their
advice and comments during the development of this book:

Barbara G. Baker,
Gladstone Secondary School,
Vancouver, B.C.

Doug Craig,
Lo-Ellen Park Secondary
    School,
Sudbury, Ontario

Ed Douglas,
Springfield Secondary
    School,
Oak Bank, Manitoba

John McCuaig,
Glenforest Secondary
    School,
Mississauga, Ontario

Maureen Royle,
Peel Board of Education,
Brampton, Ontario

Virginia Smith,
Spectrum Community
    School,
Victoria, B. C.

Doug Van Hamme,
Dr. Norman Bethune
    Collegiate Institute,
Scarborough, Ontario

Berenice L. Wood,
School District #57,
Prince George, B. C.

TABLE OF CONTENTS

TABLE OF CONTENTS

• • 3. Poems on the Lighter Side   83

•• 4. Poems on the Darker Side

TABLE OF CONTENTS

•• 6. Poetry 3000   135

TABLE OF CONTENTS

•• 9. Electric Poems of the Airwaves   183

reface

Poetry is like your own heartbeat. Poetry sustains. It is an act of existence, an affirmation.

All a poem has to do is breathe.

Poems are made of words, but words meddling in silence are toneless. Words leaping from the teeth and tongue and lips have truth, texture, tone. Read these poems aloud. When you've touched the tone, you've touched the artist.

A poem, as Sir Philip Sidney wrote in 1580, is "a speaking picture." A poem is a video with a visual and an auditory track. Poems are meant to be seen by the imagination as well as heard by the ear. Good poets don't tell you. They show you with images, pictures.

Read these poems. The poets' feelings, attitudes, ideas, reactions to the human condition now await your imaginative interpretation and appreciation.

Read a poem today.

Better still,

Make your own words breathe,

Create your own speaking picture.

"Literature is news that STAYS news."

Ezra Pound

The whole world loves a story and the poems in this section have a story to tell.

In the narrative poem or ballad the most important thing is the sequence of events as they happen.

Often the narrator begins "in medias res" (in the middle of things). Sometimes the storyteller gives us only a slice of life. The poet tells us just enough. We must fill in the missing parts.

"There are two ways of coming close to poetry. One is by writing poetry.

"But as I say, there is another way to come close to poetry, fortunately, and that is in the reading of it, not as linguistics, not as history, not as anything but poetry."

Robert Frost

Bonnie George Campbell

High upon Highlands,
    And low upon Tay,
Bonnie George Campbell
    Rade out on a day.

Saddled and bridled
    And gallant rade he;
Hame cam his guid horse,
    But never cam he.

Out cam his auld mither
    Greetin' fu' sair,
And out cam his bonnie bride
    Riving her hair.

Saddled and bridled
    And booted rade he;
Toom hame cam the saddle,
    But never cam he.

"My meadow lies green,
    And my corn is unshorn,
My barn is to build,
    And my babe is unborn."

Saddled and bridled
    And booted rade he;
Toom hame cam the saddle,
    But never came he.

Anonymous

Erosion

It took the sea a thousand years,
A thousand years to trace
The granite features of this cliff,
In crag and scarp and base.

It took the sea an hour one night,
An hour of storm to place
The sculpture of these granite seams
Upon a woman's face.

E. J. Pratt

Ballad of Birmingham

(On the bombing of a church in Birmingham, Alabama, 1963)

"Mother dear, may I go downtown
Instead of out to play,
And march the streets of Birmingham
In a Freedom March today?"

"No baby, no, you may not go,
For the dogs are fierce and wild,
And clubs and hoses, guns and jails
Aren't good for a little child."

"But, mother, I won't be alone.
Other children will go with me,
And march the streets of Birmingham
To make our country free."

"No, baby, no, you may not go,
For I fear those guns will fire.
But you may go to church instead
And sing in the children's choir."

She has combed and brushed her night-dark hair,
And bathed rose petal sweet,
And drawn white gloves on her small brown hands,
And white shoes on her feet.

The mother smiled to know her child
Was in the sacred place,
But that smile was the last smile
To come upon her face.

For when she heard the explosion,
Her eyes grew wet and wild.
She raced through the streets of Birmingham
Calling for her child.

She clawed through bits of glass and brick,
Then lifted out a shoe.
"Oh, here's the shoe my baby wore,
But, baby, where are you?"

Dudley Randall

19

Legend

The blacksmith's boy went out with a rifle
and a black dog running behind.
Cobwebs snatched at his feet,
rivers hindered him,
thorn branches caught at his eyes to make him blind
and the sky turned into an unlucky opal,
but he didn't mind,
I can break branches, I can swim rivers, I can stare out
        any spider I meet,
said he to his dog and his rifle.

The blacksmith's boy went over the paddocks
with his old black hat on his head.
Mountains jumped in his way,
rocks rolled down on him,
and the old crow cried, You'll soon be dead.
And the rain came down like mattocks.
But he only said
I can climb mountains, I can dodge rocks, I can shoot
        an old crow any day,
and he went on over the paddocks.

When he came to the end of the day the sun began falling.
Up came the night ready to swallow him,
like the barrel of a gun,
like an old black hat,
like a black dog hungry to follow him.
Then the pigeon, the magpie and the dove began wailing
and the grass lay down to billow him.
His rifle broke, his hat flew away and his dog was gone
and the sun was falling.

But in front of the night the rainbow stood on a mountain,
just as his heart foretold.
He ran like a hare,
he climbed like a fox;
he caught it in his hands, the colour and the cold—
like a bar of ice, like the column of a fountain,
like a ring of gold.
The pigeon, the magpie and the dove flew up to stare,
and the grass stood up again on the mountain.

The blacksmith's boy hung the rainbow on his shoulder
instead of his broken gun.
Lizards ran out to see,
snakes made way for him,
and the rainbow shone as brightly as the sun.
All the world said, Nobody is braver, nobody is bolder,
nobody else has done
anything to equal it. He went home as bold as he could be
with the swinging rainbow on his shoulder.

Judith Wright

In medias res—to begin "in the middle of things." We just enter the story anywhere and pick up the gist of the tale.

Edward, Edward

"Why does your brand sae drop wi' blude,
    Edward, Edward?
Why does your brand sae drop wi' blude,
    And why sae sad gang ye, O?"
"O I hae killed my hawk sae gude,
    Mither, mither:
O I hae killed my hawk sae gude,
    And I had nae mair but he, O."

"Your hawk's blude was never sae red,
    Edward, Edward.
Your hawk's blude was never sae red,
    My dear son, I tell thee, O."
"O I hae killed my red-roan steed,
    Mither, Mither:
O I hae killed my red-roan steed,
    That erst was sae fair and free, O."

"Your steed was auld, and ye hae got mair,
    Edward, Edward:
Your steed was auld, and ye hae got mair,
    Some other dule ye dree, O."
"O I hae killed my father dear,
    Mither, mither:
O I hae killed my father dear,
    Alas! and wae is me, O."

"And whatten penance will ye dree for that,
    Edward, Edward?
And whatten penance will ye dree for that?
    My dear son, now tell me, O."
"I'll set my feet in yonder boat,
    Mither, mither:
I'll set my feet in yonder boat,
    And I'll fare over the sea, O."

"And what will ye do wi' your towers and your ha',
    Edward, Edward?
And what will ye do wi' your towers and your ha'
    That were sae fair to see, O?"
"I'll let them stand till they doun fa',
    Mither, mither:
I'll let them stand till they doun fa',
    For here never mair maun I be, O."

"And what will ye leave to your bairns and your wife,
    Edward, Edward?
And what will ye leave to your bairns and your wife,
    When ye gang over the sea, O?"
"The warld's room, let them beg through life,
    Mither, mither:
The warld's room, let them beg through life,
    For them never mair will I see, O."

"And what will ye leave to your ain mither dear,
    Edward, Edward?
And what will ye leave to your ain mither dear?
    My dear son, now tell me, O."
"The curse of hell frae me sall ye bear,
    Mither, mither:
The curse of hell frae me sall ye bear,
    Sic counsels ye gave to me, O."

Anonymous

La Belle Dame Sans Merci

"O what can ail thee, knight-at-arms,
 Alone and palely loitering?
The sedge is withered from the lake,
 And no birds sing.

"O what can ail thee, knight-at-arms,
 So haggard and so woe-begone?
The squirrel's granary is full,
 And the harvest's done.

"I see a lily on thy brow
 With anguish moist and fever dew;
And on thy cheek a fading rose
 Fast withereth too."

"I met a lady in the meads,
 Full beautiful—a faery's child,
Her hair was long, her foot was light,
 And her eyes were wild.

"I made a garland for her head,
 And bracelets too, and fragrant zone;
She looked at me as she did love,
 And made sweet moan.

"I set her on my pacing steed
 And nothing else saw all day long.
For sideways would she lean, and sing
 A faery's song.

"She found me roots of relish sweet,
    And honey wild and manna dew,
And sure in language strange she said,
    'I love thee true!'

"She took me to her elfin grot,
    And there she wept and sighed full sore;
And there I shut her wild wild eyes
    With kisses four.

"And there she lullèd me asleep,
    And there I dreamed—Ah! woe betide!
The latest dream I ever dreamed
    On the cold hill side.

"I saw pale kings and princes too,
    Pale warriors, death-pale were they all;
Who cried—'La Belle Dame sans Merci
    Hath thee in thrall!"

"I saw their starved lips in the gloom
    With horrid warning gapèd wide,
And I awoke and found me here
    On the cold hill side.

"And this is why I sojourn here
    Alone and palely loitering,
Though the sedge is withered from the lake,
    And no birds sing."

John Keats

25

The Battle of Blenheim

It was a summer evening;
    Old Kaspar's work was done,
And he before his cottage door
    Was sitting in the sun;
And by him sported on the green
His little grandchild Wilhelmine.

She saw her brother Peterkin
    Roll something large and round,
Which he beside the rivulet
    In playing there had found.
He came to ask what he had found,
That was so large, and smooth, and round.

Old Kaspar took it from the boy,
    Who stood expectant by;
And then the old man shook his head,
    And with a natural sigh,
"'Tis some poor fellow's skull," said he,
"Who fell in the great victory.

"I find them in the garden,
    For there's many here about;
And often, when I go to plough,
    The ploughshare turns them out;
For many thousand men," said he,
"Were slain in that great victory."

"Now tell us what 'twas all about,"
    Young Peterkin, he cries;
And little Wilhelmine looks up
    With wonder-waiting eyes;
"Now tell us all about the war,
And what they fought each other for."

"It was the English," Kaspar said,
    "Who put the French to rout;
But what they fought each other for,

I could not well make out;
But everybody said," quoth he,
"That 'twas a famous victory.

"My father lived at Blenheim then,
    Yon little stream hard by;
They burnt his dwelling to the ground,
    And he was forced to fly;
So with his wife and child he fled,
Nor had he where to rest his head.

"With fire and sword the country round
    Was wasted far and wide,
And many a childing mother then,
    And new-born baby, died;
But things like that, you know, must be
At every famous victory.

"They say it was a shocking sight
    After the field was won;
For many thousand bodies here
    Lay rotting in the sun;
But things like that, you know, must be
After a famous victory.

"Great praise the Duke of Marlbro' won,
    And our good Prince Eugene."
"Why, 'twas a very wicked thing!"
    Said little Wilhelmine.
"Nay, nay, my little girl," quoth he,
"It was a famous victory.

"And everybody praised the Duke
    Who this great fight did win."
"But what good came of it at last?"
    Quoth little Peterkin.
"Why, that I cannot tell," said he;
"But 'twas a famous victory."

Robert Southey

Incident of the French Camp

You know, we French stormed Ratisbon:
    A mile or so away,
On a little mound, Napoleon
    Stood on our storming-day;
With neck out-thrust, you fancy how,
    Legs wide, arms locked behind,
As if to balance the prone brow
    Oppressive with its mind.

Just as perhaps he mused, "My plans
    That soar, to earth may fall,
Let once my army-leader Lannes
    Waver at yonder wall,"—
Out 'twixt the battery smokes there flew
    A rider, bound on bound
Full-galloping; nor bridle drew
    Until he reached the mound.

Then off there flung in smiling joy,
    And held himself erect
By just his horse's mane, a boy:
    You hardly could suspect—
(So tight he kept his lips compressed,
    Scarce any blood came through)
You looked twice ere you saw his breast
    Was all but shot in two.

"Well," cried he, "Emperor, by God's grace
    We've got you Ratisbon!
The Marshal's in the market-place;
    And you'll be there anon
To see your flag-bird flap his vans
    Where I, to heart's desire,
Perched him!" The Chief's eye flashed; his plans
    Soared up again like fire.

The Chief's eye flashed; but presently
    Softened itself,—as sheathes
A film the mother-eagle's eye
    When her bruised eaglet breathes:
"You're wounded!" "Nay," the soldier's pride
    Touched to the quick, he said:
"I'm killed, Sire!" And, his chief beside,
    Smiling, the boy fell dead.

Robert Browning

equiem for the Croppies

The pockets of our great coats full of barley—
No kitchens on the run, no striking camp—
We moved quick and sudden in our own country.
The priest lay behind ditches with the tramp.
A people, hardly marching—on the hike—
We found new tactics happening each day:
We'd cut through reins and rider with the pike
And stampede cattle into infantry,
Then retreat through hedges where cavalry must be thrown.
Until, on Vinegar Hill, the fatal conclave.
Terraced thousands died, shaking scythes at cannon.
The hillside blushed, soaked in our broken wave.
They buried us without shroud or coffin
And in August the barley grew up out of the grave.

Seamus Heaney

Personification — to give human characteristics
and qualities to inanimate objects, animals, or
abstract ideas.

On the Way to the Mission

They dogged him all one afternoon,
Through the bright snow,
Two whitemen servants of greed;
He knew that they were there,
But he turned not his head;
He was an Indian trapper;
He planted his snow-shoes firmly,
He dragged the long toboggan
Without rest.

10   The three figures drifted
Like shadows in the mind of a seer;
The snow-shoes were whisperers
On the threshold of awe;
The toboggan made the sound of wings,
A wood-pigeon sloping to her nest.

The Indian's face was calm.
He strode with the sorrow of fore-knowledge,
But his eyes were jewels of content
Set in circles of peace.

20   They would have shot him;
But momently in the deep forest,
They saw something flit by his side:
Their hearts stopped with fear.
Then the moon rose.

They would have left him to the spirit,
But they saw the long toboggan
Rounded well with furs,
With many a silver fox-skin,
With the pelts of mink and of otter.

30   They were the servants of greed;
When the moon grew brighter
And the spruces were dark with sleep,
They shot him.
When he fell on a shield of moonlight
One of his arms clung to his burden;
The snow was not melted:
The spirit passed away.

Then the servants of greed
Tore off the cover to count their gains;
40   They shuddered away into the shadows,
Hearing each the loud heart of the other.
Silence was born.

There in the tender moonlight,
    As sweet as they were in life,
Glimmered the ivory features,
    Of the Indian's wife.

In the manner of Montagnais women
    Her hair was rolled with braid;
Under her waxen fingers
50   A crucifix was laid.

He was drawing her down to the Mission,
    To bury her there in spring,
When the bloodroot comes and the windflower
    To silver everything.

But as a gift of plunder
    Side by side were they laid,
The moon went on to her setting
    And covered them with shade.

Duncan Campbell Scott

Funeral

When Bubby died
the whole world turned
into a splendid adventure
and everybody cried buckets
as they should've
especially the red eyed aunts
and the neighbourly wives
and twisted Norman who didn't
once all week long nasal any
10   Hank Snow songs from his happy
high flying swing
and people gathered together
in lovely little groups
around Mr. Rideout's confectionery store
and wondered whispering why he died
and little Gary Keough
who was with him when it happened
said secretly that the bogey man
pushed him over the cliff
20   and Mrs. Borden said loud enough
for his mother to hear
that he was a miserable little liar
and that he probably pushed him
over himself and some people said
it was just an accident most likely
and a very sad sad one too
him being only five and a half
and deaf 'n dumb all his little life
and Mr. Pelley said he got some fright
30   when he pulled him from the water

because he thought he was just a old onion bag
and he said he got a terrible fright
when it turned out to be Bubby
and there was never a sadder
more wonderful wake than Bubby's
because he was afterall my dead friend
who I used to play with
just about every day
including the day he died
40   and his funeral when they threw
handfuls of dirt in on top
of the sparkling white coffin
was the most glorious sad thing
in the whole whopping wide world
and nobody in all of Buckle's Valley
talked of anything else
for the most marvellous long time
until little Jimmy Pinsent
got run over by his father's truck
50   and he died too.

Al Pittman

Impressionism — The emphasis is not on
objective reality but rather on the impressions
and feelings that a scene, a person, an event
has had on the artist.

from **T**his One's on Me

my father managed a theatre

which one day (childhood reminiscence indicated) passing
on a Sunday ride, we found
the burglar alarm was ring
alingaling
out jumped my father and ran for the front door
Uncle Louie ran for the back
siren scream down the cartrack Danforth
and churchbells ding dong ding
10   (ting a ling)
and brakescreech whooee
six fat squadcars filled with the finest
of the force of our fair city
brass button boot refulgent
and in their plainclothes too
greysuit felthat and flat black footed
and arrested Uncle Louie

Oh what a brannigan
what a brouhaha
20   while Mother and Aunt Gittel and me
sat in the car and shivered
delicious
ly

because a mouse bit through a wire.

Phyllis Gotlieb

Square Dancing

We line up to do the Grand March
girls on one side
boys on the other
and begin to pair off.
The line gets shorter and shorter
and I find myself face to face with my partner,
    The Feeler.
He smiles a
lecherous smile
10   and offers me his arm.
Watching his hands carefully
I start to dance.
Is it me
or is he
holding me
a bit too close?
I realize I'm being too paranoid.
After all, I only have the word of
    ten other girls.
20   Everyone deserves a chance
to prove they're not…
The hand starts sliding
upwards from waist
past my ribs
until it is resting on
my bust.
I apologize
for accidentally hitting him in the eye
with my elbow.
30   "Switch partners!"
the gym teacher calls out.
I turn gratefully to my left
only to find that my new partner is
    The Pincher.

Shari Chudy

Television-Movie

The monster is loose.
This is an emergency area.
Leave your homes.
There is no time
to gather your belongings.
The highways are jammed,
the trains, derailed.
The planes have crashed
and the bridges are collapsing.
10   There is no escape.

Aunt Harriet has fallen down,
trying to escape.
The baby is hysterical.
The radio's broken.
The neighbours are gone.
Susie forgot her doll.
I can't find the insurance papers.
The monster has knocked over
the Tower of London.
20   The Empire State Building
is breaking in half.
Everyone is drowning
in Times Square.

In Tokyo
all the poor people
have fallen into a crevasse
which is now closing up,
even on United States citizens.
The ship's piano is rolling
30   across the ballroom floor.
The cargo is crushing the coolies.
The Army is out of ammunition.

The President has declared
a national state of affairs.
The almanacs were wrong.
The computers were in error.
Where will it all end?

The baby has stopped crying.
You hold her now; I'm tired.
40   Aunt Harriet wants to stay
one more week.
I can't say no. You tell her.
The radio repairman will come for sure
—if he can make it.
The neighbours said it's too loud.
Fix Susie's doll; the squeak's gone.
The insurance papers
are in the bottom left-hand drawer
right where you put them.
50   If they're not there,
keep looking.
Will you get paid tomorrow?
Did you mail my letter?
Did you set the alarm?

The monster is dead.
He is never coming back.
And if he does come,
someone will kill it.
And we will go on
60   just like always.
There is no escape.

Kirby Congdon

Flannan Isle

Though three men dwell on Flannan Isle
To keep the lamp alight,
As we steered under the lee we caught
No glimmer through the night.

A passing ship at dawn had brought
The news; and quickly we set sail,
To find out what strange thing might ail
The keepers of the deep-sea light.

The winter day broke blue and bright
10   With glancing sun and glancing spray,
As o'er the swell our boat made way,
As gallant as a gull in flight.

But, as we neared the lonely Isle
And looked up at the naked height
And saw the lighthouse towering white
With blinded lantern that all night
Had never shot a spark
Of comfort through the dark,
So ghostly in the cold sunlight
20   It seemed, that we were struck the while
With wonder all too dread for words.
And as into the tiny creek
We stole, beneath the hanging crag
We saw three queer, black, ugly birds—
Too big by far in my belief,
For guillemot or shag—
Like seamen sitting bolt-upright
Upon a half-tide reef:
But as we neared they plunged from sight
30   Without a sound, or spurt of white.

And still too mazed to speak,
We landed and made fast the boat
And climbed the track in single file,
Each wishing he was safe afloat
On any sea, however far,

So it be far from Flannan Isle:
And still we seemed to climb and climb
As though we'd lost all count of time
And so must climb for evermore;
40   Yet, all too soon we reached the door—
The black, sun-blistered, lighthouse door,
That gaped for us ajar.

As on the threshold for a spell
We paused, we seemed to breathe the smell
Of limewash and of tar,
Familiar as our daily breath,
As though 'twere some strange scent of death:
And so, yet wondering, side by side
We stood a moment, still tongue-tied,
50   And each with black foreboding eyed
The door, ere we should fling it wide
To leave the sunlight for the gloom:
Till, plucking courage up, at last
Hard on each other's heels we passed
Into the living-room.

Yet as we crowded through the door,
We only saw a table spread
For dinner, meat and cheese and bread;
But all untouched; and no one there,
60   As though when they sat down to eat,
Ere they could even taste,
Alarm had come, and they in haste
Had risen and left the bread and meat:
For at the table-head a chair
Lay tumbled on the floor.
We listened, but we only heard
The feeble cheeping of a bird
That starved upon its perch;
And, listening still, without a word
70   We set about our hopeless search.

We hunted high, we hunted low,
We soon ransacked the empty house;
Then o'er the Island, to and fro
We ranged, to listen and to look

In every cranny, cleft, or nook
That might have hid a bird or mouse:
But though we searched from shore to shore
We found no sign in any place,
And soon again stood face to face
80   Before the gaping door,
And stole into the room once more
As frightened children steal.

Ay, though we hunted high and low
And hunted everywhere,
Of the three men's fate we found no trace
Of any kind in any place,
But a door ajar, and an untouched meal,
And an overtoppled chair.
And, as we listened in the gloom
90   Of that forsaken living-room—
A chill clutch on our breath—
We thought how ill-chance came to all
Who kept the Flannan Light;
And how the rock had been the death
Of many a likely lad—
How six had come to a sudden end
And three had gone stark mad,
And one, whom we'd all known as friend,
Had leapt from the lantern one still night,
100   And fallen dead by the lighthouse wall—
And long we thought
On the three we sought,
And of what might yet befall.

Like curs a glance has brought to heel
We listened, flinching there,
And looked and looked on the untouched meal
And the overtoppled chair.

We seemed to stand for an endless while,
Though still no word was said,
110   Three men alive on Flannan Isle,
Who thought on three men dead.

Wilfrid Wilson Gibson

The Death of the Hired Man

Mary sat musing on the lamp-flame at the table
Waiting for Warren. When she heard his step,
She ran on tip-toe down the darkened passage
To meet him in the doorway with the news
And put him on his guard. "Silas is back."
She pushed him outward with her through the door
And shut it after her. "Be kind," she said.
She took the market things from Warren's arms
And set them on the porch, then drew him down
10   To sit beside her on the wooden steps.

"When was I ever anything but kind to him?
But I'll not have the fellow back," he said.
"I told him so last haying, didn't I?
'If he left then,' I said, 'that ended it.'
What good is he? Who else will harbour him
At his age for the little he can do?
What help he is there's no depending on.
Off he goes always when I need him most.
'He thinks he ought to earn a little pay,
20   Enough at least to buy tobacco with,
So he won't have to beg and be beholden.'
'All right,' I say, 'I can't afford to pay
Any fixed wages, though I wish I could.'
'Some one else can.' 'Then some one else will have to.'
I shouldn't mind his bettering himself
If that was what it was. You can be certain,
When he begins like that, there's some one at him
Trying to coax him off with pocketmoney,—
In haying time, when any help is scarce.
30   In winter he comes back to us. I'm done."

"Sh! not so loud: he'll hear you," Mary said.

"I want him to: he'll have to soon or late."

"He's worn out. He's asleep beside the stove.
When I came up from Rowe's I found him here,
Huddled against the barn-door fast asleep,

A miserable sight, and frightening, too—
You needn't smile—I didn't recognize him—

I wasn't looking for him—and he's changed.
Wait till you see."

40   "Where did you say he'd been?"

"He didn't say. I dragged him to the house,
And gave him tea and tried to make him smoke.
I tried to make him talk about his travels.
Nothing would do: he just kept nodding off."

"What did he say? Did he say anything?"

"But little."

         "Anything? Mary, confess
He said he'd come to ditch the meadow for me."

"Warren!"

50   "But did he? I just want to know."

"Of course he did. What would you have him say?
Surely you wouldn't grudge the poor old man
Some humble way to save his self-respect.
He added, if you really care to know,
He meant to clear the upper pasture, too.
That sounds like something you have heard before?
Warren, I wish you could have heard the way
He jumbled everything. I stopped to look
Two or three times—he made me feel so queer—
60   To see if he was talking in his sleep.
He ran on Harold Wilson—you remember—
The boy you had in haying four years since.
He's finished school, and teaching in his college.
Silas declares you'll have to get him back.
He says they two will make a team for work:
Between them they will lay this farm as smooth!
The way he mixed that in with other things.
He thinks young Wilson a likely lad, though daft
On education—you know how they fought
70   All through July under the blazing sun,

Silas up on the cart to build the load,
Harold along beside to pitch it on."

"Yes, I took care to keep well out of earshot."

"Well, those days trouble Silas like a dream.
You wouldn't think they would. How some things linger!
Harold's young college boy's assurance piqued him.
After so many years he still keeps finding
Good arguments he sees he might have used.
I sympathize. I know just how it feels
80   To think of the right thing to say too late.
Harold's associated in his mind with Latin.
He asked me what I thought of Harold's saying
He studied Latin like the violin
Because he liked it—that an argument!
He said he couldn't make the boy believe
He could find water with a hazel prong—
Which showed how much good school had ever done him.
He wanted to go over that. But most of all
He thinks if he could have another chance
90   To teach him how to build a load of hay—"

"I know, that's Silas' one accomplishment.
He bundles every forkful in its place,
And tags and numbers it for future reference,
So he can find and easily dislodge it
In the unloading. Silas does that well.
He takes it out in bunches like big birds' nests.
You never see him standing on the hay
He's trying to lift, straining to lift himself."

"He thinks if he could teach him that, he'd be
100   Some good perhaps to some one in the world.
He hates to see a boy the fool of books.
Poor Silas, so concerned for other folk,
And nothing to look backward to with pride,
And nothing to look forward to with hope,
So now and never any different."

Part of a moon was falling down the west,
Dragging the whole sky with it to the hills.
Its light poured softly in her lap. She saw

And spread her apron to it. She put out her hand
110   Among the harp-like morning-glory strings,
Taut with the dew from garden bed to eaves,
As if she played unheard the tenderness
That wrought on him beside her in the night.
"Warren," she said, "he has come home to die:
You needn't be afraid he'll leave you this time."

"Home," he mocked gently.

                    "Yes, what else but home?
It all depends on what you mean by home.
Of course he's nothing to us, any more
120   Than was the hound that came a stranger to us
Out of the woods, worn out upon the trail."

"Home is the place where, when you have to go there,
They have to take you in."

                "I should have called it
Something you somehow haven't to deserve."

Warren leaned out and took a step or two,
Picked up a little stick and brought it back
And broke it in his hand and tossed it by.
"Silas has better claim on us you think
130   Than on his brother? Thirteen little miles
As the road winds would bring him to his door.
Silas has walked that far no doubt today.
Why didn't he go there? His brother's rich,
A somebody—director in the bank."

"He never told us that."

              "We know it though."

"I think his brother ought to help, of course.
I'll see to that if there is need. He ought of right
To take him in, and might be willing to—
140   He may be better than appearances.
But have some pity on Silas. Do you think
If he'd had any pride in claiming kin
Or anything he looked for from his brother,
He'd keep so still about him all this time?"

"I wonder what's between them."

                                          "I can tell you.
Silas is what he is—we wouldn't mind him—
But just the kind that kinsfolk can't abide.
He never did a thing so very bad.

150   He don't know why he isn't quite as good
As any one. He won't be made ashamed
To please his brother, worthless though he is."

"I can't think Si ever hurt any one."

"No, but he hurt my heart the way he lay
And rolled his old head on that sharp-edged chair-back.
He wouldn't let me put him on the lounge.
You must go in and see what you can do.
I made the bed up for him there tonight.
You'll be surprised at him—how much he's broken.

160   His working days are done; I'm sure of it."

"I'd not be in a hurry to say that."

"I haven't been. Go, look, see for yourself.
But, Warren, please remember how it is:
He's come to help you ditch the meadow.
He has a plan. You mustn't laugh at him.
He may not speak of it and then he may.
I'll sit and see if that small sailing cloud
Will hit or miss the moon."

                                   It hit the moon.

170   Then there were three there, making a dim row,
The moon, the little silver cloud, and she.

Warren returned—too soon, it seemed to her,
Slipped to her side, caught up her hand and waited.

"Warren," she questioned.

                                  "Dead," was all he answered.

Robert Frost

Dialogue poem — the poem takes the form and rhythm of a conversation.

hat Do I Remember of the Evacuation?

What do I remember of the evacuation?
I remember my father telling Tim and me
About the mountains and the train
And the excitement of going on a trip.
What do I remember of the evacuation?
I remember my mother wrapping
A blanket around me and my
Pretending to fall asleep so she would be happy
Although I was so excited I couldn't sleep
(I hear there were people herded
Into the Hastings Park like cattle.
Families were made to move in two hours
Abandoning everything, leaving pets
And possessions at gun point.
I hear families were broken up
Men were forced to work. I heard
It whispered late at night
That there was suffering) and
I missed my dolls.
What do I remember of the evacuation?
I remember Miss Foster and Miss Tucker
Who still live in Vancouver
And who did what they could
And loved the children and who gave me
A puzzle to play with on the train.

10

20

And I remember the mountains and I was
Six years old and I swear I saw a giant
Gulliver of Gulliver's Travels scanning the horizon
And when I told my mother she believed it too
30   And I remember how careful my parents were
Not to bruise us with bitterness
And I remember the puzzle of Lorraine Life
Who said "Don't insult me" when I
Proudly wrote my name in Japanese
And Tim flew the Union Jack
When the war was over but Lorraine
And her friends spat on us anyway
and I prayed to the God who loves
All the children in his sight
40   That I might be white.

Joy Kogawa

Free verse — the poet follows the natural
cadences of the language and discards traditional
metre, rhyme, and stanza patterns.

The Cremation of Sam McGee

There are strange things done in the midnight sun
  By the men who moil for gold;
The Arctic trails have their secret tales
  That would make your blood run cold;
The Northern Lights have seen queer sights,
  But the queerest they ever did see
Was that night on the marge of Lake Lebarge
  I cremated Sam McGee.

Now Sam McGee was from Tennessee, where the
    cotton blooms and blows.
Why he left his home in the South to roam round
    the Pole, God only knows.
He was always cold, but the land of gold seemed to
    hold him like a spell;
Though he'd often say in his homely way that he'd
    "sooner live in hell."

On a Christmas day we were mushing our way over
    the Dawson trail.
Talk of your cold! through the parka's fold it stabbed
    like a driven nail.
If our eyes we'd close, then the lashes froze till
    sometimes we couldn't see;
It wasn't much fun, but the only one to whimper
    was Sam McGee.

And that very night, as we lay packed tight in our
    robes beneath the snow,
And the dogs were fed, and the stars o'erhead were
    dancing heel and toe,
He turned to me, and "Cap," says he, "I'll cash in
    this trip, I guess;
And if I do, I'm asking you that you won't refuse
    my last request."

Well, he seemed so low that I couldn't say no; then
      he says with a sort of moan:
"It's the cursèd cold, and it's got right hold till I'm
      chilled clean through to the bone.
Yet 'tain't being dead—it's my awful dread of the
      icy grave that pains;
So I want you to swear that, foul or fair, you'll
      cremate my last remains."

A pal's last need is a thing to heed, so I swore
      I would not fail;
And so we started on at streak of dawn; but God!
      he looked ghastly pale.
He crouched on the sleigh and he raved all day of
      his home in Tennessee;
And before nightfall a corpse was all that was left
      of Sam McGee.

There wasn't a breath in that land of death, and
      I hurried, horror-driven,
With a corpse half-hid that I could get rid, because
      of a promise given;
It was lashed to the sleigh, and it seemed to say:
      "You may tax your brawn and brains,
But you promised true, and it's up to you to cremate
      these last remains."

Now a promise made is a debt unpaid, and the trail
      has its own stern code.
In the days to come, though my lips were dumb, in
      my heart how I cursed that load.
In the long, long night, by the lone fire-light, while
      the huskies round in a ring,
Howled out their woes to the homeless snows—
      O God! how I loathed the thing!

And every day that quiet clay seemed to heavy and
    heavier grow;
And on I went, though the dogs were spent and the
    grub was getting low;
The trail was bad, and I felt half mad, but I swore
    I would not give in;
And I'd often sing to the hateful thing, and it
    hearkened with a grin.

Till I came to the marge of Lake Lebarge, and a
    derelict there lay;
It was jammed in the ice, and I saw in a trice it was
    called the *Alice May*.
And I looked at it, and I thought a bit, and I looked
    at my frozen chum;
Then "Here," said I, with a sudden cry, "is my
    cre-ma-tor-eum."

Some planks I tore from the cabin floor, and I lit the
    boiler fire;
Some coal I found that was lying around, and I
    heaped the fuel higher;
The flames just soared, and the furnace roared—such
    a blaze you seldom see;
And I burrowed a hole in the glowing coal, and I
    stuffed in Sam McGee.

Then I made a hike, for I didn't like to hear him
    sizzle so;
And the heavens scowled, and the huskies howled,
    and the wind began to blow.
It was icy cold, but the hot sweat rolled down my
    cheeks, and I don't know why;
And the greasy smoke in an inky cloak went streaking
    down the sky.

I do not know how long in the snow I wrestled with
    grisly fear;
But the stars came out and they danced about ere
    again I ventured near;
I was sick with dread, but I bravely said: "I'll just
    take a peep inside.
I guess he's cooked, and it's time I looked,"…then
    the door I opened wide.

And there sat Sam, looking cool and calm, in the
    heart of the furnace roar;
And he wore a smile you could see a mile, and he
    said: "Please close that door.
It's fine in here, but I greatly fear you'll let in the
    cold and storm—
Since I left Plumtree, down in Tennessee, it's the
    first time I've been warm."

There are strange things done in the midnight sun
    By the men who moil for gold;
The Arctic trails have their secret tales
    That would make your blood run cold;
The Northern Lights have seen queer sights,
    But the queerest they ever did see
Was that night on the marge of Lake Lebarge
    I cremated Sam McGee.

Robert Service

The Highwayman

Part I

The wind was a torrent of darkness
among the gusty trees,
The moon was a ghostly galleon tossed upon
cloudy seas,
The road was a ribbon of moonlight over
the purple moor,
And the highwayman came riding—
Riding—riding—
The highwayman came riding, up to the old inn-door.

He'd a French cocked-hat on his forehead, a bunch
of lace at his chin,
A coat of the claret velvet, and breeches
of brown doeskin;
They fitted with never a wrinkle: his boots were
up to the thigh!
And he rode with a jewelled twinkle,
His pistol butts a-twinkle,
His rapier hilt a-twinkle, under the jewelled sky.

Over the cobbles he clattered and clashed in the
dark inn-yard,
And he tapped with his whip on the shutters, but all
was locked and barred;
He whistled a tune to the window, and who should
be waiting there
But the landlord's black-eyed daughter,
Bess, the landlord's daughter,
Plaiting a dark red love-knot into her long black hair.

And dark in the dark old inn-yard a stable wicket
creaked
Where Tim the ostler listened; his face was white
and peaked;
His eyes were hollows of madness, his hair like
mouldy hay,

But he loved the landlord's daughter,
  The landlord's red-lipped daughter;
Dumb as a dog he listened, and he heard the robber say—

"One kiss, by bonny sweetheart, I'm after a prize
    tonight,
But I shall be back with the yellow gold before
    the morning light;
Yet, if they press me sharply, and harry me through
    the day,
Then look for me by moonlight,
  Watch for me by moonlight,
I'll come to thee by moonlight, though hell should
    bar the way."

He rose upright in the stirrups; he scarce could
    reach her hand,
But she loosened her hair i' the casement! His face burnt
    like a brand
As the black cascade of perfume came tumbling
    over his breast;
And he kissed its waves in the moonlight,
  (Oh, sweet black waves in the moonlight!)
Then he tugged at his rein in the moonlight, and
    galloped away to the west.

Part II

He did not come in the dawning; he did not come
    at noon;
And out o' the tawny sunset, before the rise
    o' the moon,
When the road was a gypsy's ribbon, looping
    the purple moor,
A red-coat troop came marching—
  Marching—marching—
King George's men came marching, up to the old inn-door.

They said no word to the landlord, they drank
    his ale instead,
But they gagged his daughter and bound her
    to the foot of her narrow bed;
Two of them knelt at her casement, with muskets
    at their side!
There was death at every window;
   And hell at one dark window;
For Bess could see, through her casement, the road
    that *he* would ride.

They had tied her up to attention, with many
    a sniggering jest;
They had bound a musket beside her, with the barrel
    beneath her breast!
"Now keep good watch!" and they kissed her. She
    heard the dead man say—
Look for me by moonlight;
   Watch for me by moonlight;
I'll come to thee by moonlight, though hell should bar the way!

She twisted her hands behind her; but all the knots
    held good!
She writhed her hands till her fingers were wet
    with sweat or blood!
They stretched and strained in the darkness, and
    the hours crawled by like years,
Till now, on the stroke of midnight,
   Cold, on the stroke of midnight,
The tip of one finger touched it! The trigger at least
    was hers!

The tip of one finger touched it; she strove no more
    for the rest!
Up, she stood at attention, with the barrel beneath
    her breast,
She would not risk their hearing; she would not
    strive again;

For the road lay bare in the moonlight;
  Blank and bare in the moonlight;
And the blood in her veins in the moonlight throbbed
    to her love's refrain.

Tlot-tlot; *tlot-tlot!* Had they heard it? The horse-hoofs
    ringing clear;
Tlot-tlot, *tlot-tlot*, in the distance? Were they deaf
    that they did not hear?
Down the ribbon of moonlight, over the brow
    of the hill,
The highwayman came riding,
  Riding, riding!
The red-coats looked to their priming! She stood up,
    straight and still!

Tlot-tlot, in the frosty silence! *Tlot-tlot*, in the
    echoing night!
Nearer he came and nearer! Her face was like a light!
Her eyes grew wide for a moment; she drew one
    last deep breath,
Then her finger moved in the moonlight,
  Her musket shattered the moonlight,
Shattered her breast in the moonlight and warned
    him—with her death.

He turned; he spurred to the westward; he did not
    know who stood
Bowed, with her head o'er the musket, drenched
    with her own red blood!
Not till the dawn he heard it, and slowly blanched
    to hear
How Bess, the landlord's daughter,
  The landlord's black-eyed daughter,
Had watched for her love in the moonlight, and died
    in darkness there.

Back, he spurred like a madman, shrieking a curse
 to the sky,
With the white road smoking behind him and his
 rapier brandished high!
Blood-red were his spurs i' the golden noon, wine-red
 was his velvet coat;
When they shot him down on the highway,
 Down like a dog on the highway,
And he lay in his blood on the highway, with the
 bunch of lace at his throat.

. . . . .

And still of a winter's night, they say, when the wind
 is in the trees,
When the moon is a ghostly galleon tossed
 upon cloudy seas,
When the road is a ribbon of moonlight over
 the purple moor,
A highwayman comes riding—
 Riding—riding—
A highwayman comes riding, up to the old inn-door.

Over the cobbles he clatters and clangs in the
 dark inn-yard;
And he taps with his whip on the shutters, but all
 is locked and barred;
He whistles a tune to the window, and who should
 be waiting there
But the landlord's black-eyed daughter,
 Bess, the landlord's daughter,
Plaiting a dark red love-knot into her long black hair.

Alfred Noyes

> "Poetry is a response to the daily
> necessity of getting the world right."
>
> **Wallace Stevens**

A poet makes a comment on life around us, within us. A poet tells us who we are, where we have been, and where we might be going.

All a poem asks from us is that we come to it with an open mind. A good poem will pose its own questions. A poem worth its hire can sustain a little analysis and discussion. Press the poem for its insights and then move on.

> "A poem is not a destination, it is a point
> of departure. The destination is
> determined by the reader. The poet's
> function is but to point direction. A poem
> is not the conflagration complete, it is the
> first kindling."
>
> **A. M. Klein**

Eclipse

I looked the sun straight in the eye.
He put on dark glasses.

F. R. Scott

The Road Not Taken

Two roads diverged in a yellow wood,
And sorry I could not travel both
And be one traveller, long I stood
And looked down one as far as I could
To where it bent in the undergrowth;

Then took the other, as just as fair,
And having perhaps the better claim,
Because it was grassy and wanted wear;
Though as for that the passing there
Had worn them really about the same,

And both that morning equally lay
In leaves no step had trodden black.
Oh, I kept the first for another day!
Yet knowing how way leads on to way,
I doubted if I should ever come back.

I shall be telling this with a sigh
Somewhere ages and ages hence:
Two roads diverged in a wood, and I—
I took the one less travelled by,
And that has made all the difference.

Robert Frost

A poet pauses, reflects, and records in words his ideas, feelings, impressions.

The poet arranges her words in patterns on the page — patterns that appeal to our visual and auditory senses.

Afternoon on a Hill

I will be the gladdest thing
   Under the sun!
I will touch a hundred flowers
   And not pick one.

I will look at cliffs and clouds
   With quiet eyes,
Watch the wind bow down the grass,
   And the grass rise.

And when lights begin to show
   Up from the town,
I will mark which must be mine,
   And then start down!

Edna St. Vincent Millay

Joy Sonnet in a Random Universe

Sometimes I'm happy: la la la la la la la
la la la la la la la la la la la la la la la la
la la la la. Tum tum ti tum. La la la la la la
la la la la la la la la la la la la la la la la.
Hey nonny nonny. La la la la la la la la la
la la la la la la la la la la la. Vo do di o do.
Poo poo pi doo. La la la la la la la la la la
la la la la la la la la la la la la la la la la la
la la. Whack a doo. La la la la la la la. Sh-
boom, sh-boom. La la la la la la la la la la
la la la la la la la la la la la la la la la la la
la la. Dum di dum. La la la la la la la la la
la la la la la la la la la. Tra la la. Tra la la
la la la la la la la la la la. Yeah yeah yeah.

Helen Chasin

Cooks Brook

At the pool where we used to swim
in Cooks Brook
not everyone had guts enough
to dive from the top ledge

not that it would have been
a difficult dive
except for the shelf of rock
that lay two feet below the surface
and reached quarter of the way out
10   into the width of the pool

one by one the brave few of us
would climb the cliff to the ledge
and stand poised
ready to plunge headfirst
into the dark water below
and always there was that moment
of terror
when you'd doubt that you could
clear the shelf
20   knowing full well
it would be better to die
skull smashed open in the water
than it would be to climb
backwards down to the beach

so always there was that moment
when you prayed for wings
then sailed arms outspread into the buoyant air
what you feel is something
impossible to describe
30   as the water parts like a wound
to engulf you
then closes just as quickly
in a white scar where you entered

and you are surprised always
to find yourself alive
following the streaks of sunlight
that lead you gasping to the surface
where you make your way
leisurely to shore
40   as though there had been nothing to it
as though it was every day of the week
you daringly defied the demons
who lived so terribly
in the haunted hours of your sleep

Al Pittman

A poet selects every word in the poem with great care. A poem rests on a definite textual base.

What do the words *mean*?

What do the words *suggest*?

DENOTATION
AND
CONNOTATION

The Six Blind Men of Hindostan

It was six men of Hindostan,
  To learning much inclined,
Who went to see the elephant
  (Though all of them were blind);
That each by observation
  Might satisfy his mind.

The first approached the elephant,
  And happening to fall
Against his broad and sturdy side,
  At once began to bawl,
"Bless me, it seems the elephant
  Is very like a wall."

The second, feeling of his tusk,
  Cried, "Ho! what have we here
So very round and smooth and sharp?
  To me 'tis mighty clear
This wonder of an elephant
  Is very like a spear."

The third approached the animal,
  And happening to take
The squirming trunk within his hands,
  Then boldly up and spake;
"I see," quoth he, "the elephant
  Is very like a snake."

The fourth stretched out his eager hand
　　And felt about the knee;
"What most this mighty beast is like
　　Is mighty plain," quoth he;
"'Tis clear enough the elephant
　　Is very like a tree."

The fifth who chanced to touch the ear
　　Said, "Even the blindest man
Can tell what this resembles most;
　　Deny the fact who can,
This marvel of an elephant
　　Is very like a fan."

The sixth no sooner had begun
　　About the beast to grope
Than, seizing on the swinging tail,
　　That fell within his scope,
"I see," cried he, "the elephant
　　Is very like a rope."

And so these men of Hindostan
　　Disputed loud and long,
Each in his own opinion
　　Exceeding stiff and strong,
Though each was partly in the right,
　　And each was partly wrong.

J. G. Saxe

Reach out

and look
at this world
differently
it's easier

Upside Down

Ronald Keen

ugging

Hugging is healthy: it helps the body's immune
system, it cures depression,
it reduces stress, it induces sleep, it's invigorating,
it's rejuvenating, and it has no unpleasant side-effects.
Hugging is nothing less than a miracle drug.

Hugging is all natural: it is organic, naturally sweet,
contains no pesticides, no preservatives, no artificial
ingredients and is 100% wholesome.

Hugging is practically perfect: it has no movable
parts, no batteries to wear out, requires no periodic
check-ups, no monthly payments, has no insurance
requirements, is theft-proof, non taxable,
unpolluting and is, of course,
fully returnable.

Anonymous

What being a Strawberry means

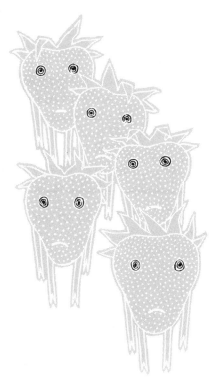

Someone said
it was an evil shape,
this fat, red
heart that grew
out of the ground,
that slept on a straw mattress
in July sawdust.

Some thought him
Cowardly, never
an exact colour.
Some thought him
Harmful, crooked
as elm-blight.

Some thought him
Carefree, a stale fume
in the sun's light.

But he was not
any of
those things.

The mass of strawberries
lead lives of quiet desperation.

Susan Musgrave

Winter Morning

All I can know
Is that I am
A human being.
What does that mean?

Two eyes, a mouth,
A carrot for a nose.
My arms are two dead twigs,
My legs a ball of snow.

Irene Cox

Poison Tree

I was angry with my friend:
I told my wrath, my wrath did end.
I was angry with my foe:
I told it not, my wrath did grow.

And I water'd it in fears,
Night and morning with my tears;
And I sunnèd it with smiles,
And with soft deceitful wiles.

And it grew both day and night,
Till it bore an apple bright;
And my foe beheld it shine,
And he knew that it was mine,

And into my garden stole
When the night had veil'd the pole:
In the morning glad I see
My foe outstretch'd beneath the tree.

William Blake

"Poets are the unacknowledged
legislators of the world."

Percy Bysshe Shelley

A good poem will sustain more than one visit.

Abou Ben Adhem

Abou Ben Adhem (may his tribe increase!)
Awoke one night from a deep dream of peace,
And saw, within the moonlight in his room,
Making it rich and like a lily in bloom,
An angel writing in a book of gold:—
Exceeding peace had made Ben Adhem bold,
And to the presence in the room he said,
"What writest thou?"—The vision raised its head,
And, with a look made of all sweet accord,
Answered, "The names of those who love the Lord."
"And is mine one?" said Abou. "Nay, not so,"
Replied the angel. Abou spoke more low,
But cheerily still, and said, "I pray thee, then,
Write me as one that loves his fellow-men."

The angel wrote, and vanished. The next night
It came again, with a great wakening light,
And showed the names whom love of God had blessed,—
And, lo! Ben Adhem's name led all the rest!

Leigh Hunt

He Sits Down on the Floor of a School for the Retarded

I sit down on the floor of a school for the retarded,
a writer of magazine articles accompanying a band
that was met at the door by a child in a man's body
who asked them. "Are you the surprise they promised us?"

It's Ryan's Fancy, Dermot on guitar,
Fergus on banjo, Denis on penny-whistle.
In the eyes of this audience, they're everybody
who has ever appeared on TV. I've been telling lies
to a boy who cried because his favourite detective
10   hadn't come with us; I said he had sent his love
and, no, I didn't think he'd mind if I signed his name
to a scrap of paper: when the boy took it, he said,
"Nobody will ever get this away from me,"
in the voice, more hopeless than defiant,
of one accustomed to finding that his hiding places
have been discovered, used to having objects snatched
out of his hands. Weeks from now I'll send him
another autograph, this one genuine
in the sense of having been signed by somebody
20   on the same payroll as the star.
Then I'll feel less ashamed. Now everyone is singing,
"Old MacDonald had a farm," and I don't know what to do

about the young woman (I call her a woman
because she's twenty-five at least, but think of her
as a little girl, she plays that part so well,
having known no other), about the young woman who
sits down beside me and, as if it were the most natural
thing in the world, rests her head on my shoulder.

It's nine o'clock in the morning, not an hour for music.
30   And, at the best of times, I'm uncomfortable
in situations where I'm ignorant
of the accepted etiquette: it's one thing
to jump a fence, quite another thing to blunder

into one in the dark. I look around me
for a teacher to whom to smile out my distress.
They're all busy elsewhere. "Hold me," she whispers. "Hold me."
I put my arm around her. "Hold me tighter."
I do, and she snuggles closer. I half-expect
someone in authority to grab her
40   or me; I can imagine this being remembered
for ever as the time the sex-crazed writer
publicly fondled the poor retarded girl.
"Hold me," she says again. What does it matter
what anybody thinks? I put my other arm around her,
rest my chin in her hair, thinking of children
real children, and of how they say it, "Hold me,"
and of a patient in a geriatric ward
I once heard crying out to his mother, dead
for half a century, "I'm frightened! Hold me!"
50   and of a boy-soldier screaming it on the beach
at Dieppe, of Nelson in Hardy's arms,
of Frieda gripping Lawrence's ankle
until he sailed off in his Ship of Death.

It's what we all want, in the end,
to be held, merely to be held,
to be kissed (not necessarily with the lips,
for every touching is a kind of kiss).

Yes, it's what we all want, in the end,
not to be worshipped, not to be admired,
60   not to be famous, not to be feared,
not even to be loved, but simply to be held.

She hugs me now, this retarded woman, and I hug her.
We are brother and sister, father and daughter,
mother and son, husband and wife.
We are lovers. We are two human beings
huddled together for a little while by the fire
in the Ice Age, two hundred thousand years ago.

Alden Nowlan

Today

today holds the tale of yesterday
and promises tomorrow
you were younger then
today you are older
tomorrow you will be older still
and yet you move on the same trails
you see the same days many times over
colours change
you grow cold and warm as you move
you bring onto me what I can take
you ask for only my life
as I wander with you
you have been a cold year

Leo Yerxa

Lullaby of the Iroquois

Little brown baby-bird, lapped in your nest,
    Wrapped in your nest,
    Strapped in your nest,
Your straight little cradle-board rocks you to rest;
    Its hands are your nest;
    Its bands are your nest;
Its swings from the down-bending branch of the oak;
You watch the camp flame, and the curling grey smoke;
But, oh, for your pretty black eyes sleep is best,—
Little brown baby of mine, go to rest.

Little brown baby-bird swinging to sleep,
    Winging to sleep,
    Singing to sleep,
Your wonder-black eyes that so wide open keep,
    Shielding their sleep,
    Unyielding to sleep,
The heron is homing, the plover is still,
The night-owl calls from his haunt on the hill,
Afar the fox barks, afar the stars peep,—
Little brown baby of mine, go to sleep.

E. Pauline Johnson

Cree Ponies

Silhouettes, they lean against a ringed moon,
their heads down against the threat of snow.
Below, in the distance
a diesel moans runs along the tracks
where dead coal cinders gather
and play out towards Calgary.

No movement. They hump against the night.
Only quivering patches of skin crack the air,
memories of summer fly off.

Mane and tail hanging vertical as ice,
they sleep dead centuries,
or if ponies dream they dream.

Below on the flat where light strikes water,
a last ember sparks out. A dog complains.

The diesel warns again, begins its roar, passes.
They raise their heads, blink,
then drop back once more into centuries or dreams.

R. A. Kawalikak

Unemployment

The chrome lid of the coffee pot
twists off, and the glass knob rinsed.
Lift out the assembly, dump
the grounds out. Wash the pot and
fill with water, put everything back with
fresh grounds and snap the top down.
Plug in again and wait.

Unemployment is also
a great snow deep around the house
choking the street, and the City.
Nothing moves. Newspaper photographs
show the traffic backed up for miles.
Going out to shovel the walk
I think how in a few days the sun will clear this.
No one will know I worked here.

This is like whatever I do.
How strange that so magnificent a thing as a body
with its twinges, its aches
should have all that chemistry, that bulk
the intricate electrical brain
subjected to something as tiny
as buying a postage stamp.
Or selling it.

Or waiting.

Tom Wayman

In Addition

In addition to the fact I lost my job for a nosebleed
In addition to the fact my unemployment insurance stamps
        were just one week short
In addition to the fact I'm standing in line at the Sally Ann for
        a breakfast of one thin baloney sandwich and coffee
In addition to all that it's lousy coffee.

Milton Acorn

Caliban in the Coal Mines

God, we don't like to complain.
    We know that the mine is no lark.
But—there's the pools from the rain;
    But—there's the cold and the dark.

God, You don't know what it is—
    You, in Your well-lighted sky—
Watching the meteors whizz;
    Warm, with a sun always by.

God, if You had but the moon
    Stuck in Your cap for a lamp,
Even You'd tire of it soon,
    Down in the dark and the damp.

Nothing but blackness above
    And nothing that moves but the cars...
God, if You wish for our love,
    Fling us a handful of stars!

Louis Untermeyer

Paper Matches

My aunts washed dishes while the uncles
squirted each other on the lawn with
    garden hoses. Why are we in here,
I said, and they are out there?
    That's the way it is,
    said Aunt Hetty, the shrivelled-up one.

I have the rages that small animals have,
being small, being animal.
    Written on me was a message,
"At Your Service," like a book of
paper matches. One by one we were
taken out and struck.
    We come bearing supper,
our heads on fire.

Paulette Jiles

Provide, Provide!

The witch that came (the withered hag)
To wash the steps with pail and rag,
Was once the beauty Abishag,

The picture pride of Hollywood.
Too many fall from great and good
For you to doubt the likelihood.

Die early and avoid the fate.
Or if predestined to die late,
Make up your mind to die in state.

Make the whole stock exchange your own!
If need be occupy a throne,
Where nobody can call *you* crone.

Some have relied on what they knew,
Others on being simply true.
What worked for them might work for you.

No memory of having starred
Atones for later disregard
Or keeps the end from being hard.

Better to go down dignified
With boughten friendship at your side
Than none at all. Provide, provide!

Robert Frost

Tercet — a three-line stanza in
rhyming triplets (a a a b b b c c c).

The Lamentation of the Old Pensioner

Although I shelter from the rain
Under a broken tree,
My chair was nearest to the fire
In every company
That talked of love or politics,
Ere Time transfigured me.

Though lads are making pikes again
For some conspiracy,
And crazy rascals rage their fill
At human tyranny,
My contemplations are of Time
That has transfigured me.

There's not a woman turns her face
Upon a broken tree,
And yet the beauties that I loved
Are in my memory;
I spit into the face of Time
That has transfigured me.

William Butler Yeats

When I chance to think of my childhood

and recall all the old memories from those days,

then youth seems a time

when all meat was juicy and tender,

and no game too swift for the hunter.

Now, I have only the old stories

and songs to fall back upon.

traditional Inuit song

from Auguries of Innocence

To see a World in a grain of sand,
And a Heaven in a wild flower,
Hold Infinity in the palm of your hand,
And Eternity in an hour.
A robin redbreast in a cage
Puts all Heaven in a rage.
A dove-house fill'd with doves and pigeons
Shudders Hell thro' all its regions.
A dog starv'd at his master's gate
10   Predicts the ruin of the State.
A horse misus'd upon the road
Calls to Heaven for human blood.
Each outcry of the hunted hare
A fibre from the brain does tear.
A skylark wounded in the wing,
A cherubim does cease to sing.
The game-cock clipt and arm'd for fight
Does the rising sun affright.
Every wolf's and lion's howl
20   Raises from Hell a Human soul.
The wild deer, wandering here and there,
Keeps the Human soul from care.
The lamb misus'd breeds public strife,
And yet forgives the butcher's knife.
The bat that flits at close of eve
Has left the brain that won't believe.
The owl that calls upon the night
Speaks the unbeliever's fright.
He who shall hurt the little wren
30   Shall never be belov'd by men.

William Blake

Rhyming couplets — two lines of poetry that rhyme.

Birds

Whatever the bird is, is perfect in the bird.
Weapon kestrel hard as a blade's curve,
thrush round as a mother or a full drop of water,
fruit-green parrot wise in his shrieking swerve—
all are what bird is and do not reach beyond bird.

Whatever the bird does is right for the bird to do—
cruel kestrel dividing in his hunger the sky,
thrush in the trembling dew beginning to sing,
parrot clinging and quarrelling and veiling his queer eye—
all these are as birds are and good for birds to do.

But I am torn and beleaguered by my own people.
The blood that feeds my heart is the blood they gave me,
and my heart is the house where they gather and fight for dominion—
all different, all with a wish and a will to save me,
to turn me into the ways of other people.

If I could leave their battleground for the forest of a bird
I could melt the past, the present and the future in one
and find the words that lie behind all these languages.
Then I could fuse my passions into one clear stone
and be simple to myself as the bird is to the bird.

Judith Wright

Instress — the instinct or pressure from within
something that urges it to pursue its proper
function. The word was created by the poet
Gerard Manley Hopkins.

Flea

this ticking child
with all its eyes opened
with all its legs held
between my fingertips
this blood relative
found on my leg
what can I do with you?
I don't believe
in even small executions
but what's to be done?
I can't talk you out of it
can't change your mind
you're nature's boy
you know what tastes good
what makes you drunk and happy.

I dig my fingernail
into its neck
its head drops
a thousand miles
to the floor

Don Domanski

Gothic — ghosts, mystery, horrible
happenings, and the macabre.

Untitled

sometimes I wonder
if all those spiders I've squished
have ghosts

Anne Malcolm

First and Last

I was born on August 4th 1945,
and on August 5th,
while I suckled in tranquility,
Hiroshima played host
to the first Atomic Bomb.
God, to think of all those people
who woke with me,
only once.

Joseph Sherman

evry whun at 2 o'clock

on saturday was quiet stayd off th
streets very few cars   i was in th
restaurant wher a guy at nothr tabul
had a portabul radio receiving from
wher th blast was gonna happn
from evrywhun listining down
to 4 - 3 - 2 - 1 - zero   its a quiet day
nd th peopul arint doing much now late
breakfast at watr level   and if th
watr cums up th street wud th
ownr let us all eat from th kitchn
for nothing hope th windows ar all closd
nd after nothin happens xcept th
peopul ar changd   th vancouvr
sun newspapr sz N-blast
successful and safe   only it
isint an all th peopul know

bill bissett

I'm Nobody! Who are you?
Are you Nobody too?
Then there's a pair of us?
Don't tell! They'd advertise, you know!

How dreary to be Somebody!
How public—like a frog—
To tell one's name the livelong June
To an admiring bog!

Emily Dickinson

Lanterns

the blizzard came
after the first frost—
the hired man left the house
with a lantern
to see how the cattle
were taking the storm
in the north pasture

my father found him
three days later
near the fence on the east side
of the pasture

the faithful dog froze
beside him—curled up

like a lover in the man's arms
(the broken lantern
lay near a stone   the glass shattered)

men freeze this way everywhere
when lanterns fall   a p a r t
(even within one's arms
inside the city's rim)

Andrew Suknaski

Uphill

Does the road wind uphill all the way?
    Yes, to the very end.
Will the day's journey take the whole long day?
    From morn to night, my friend.

But is there for the night a resting-place?
    A roof for when the slow, dark hours begin.
May not the darkness hide it from my face?
    You cannot miss that inn.

Shall I meet other wayfarers at night?
    Those who have gone before.
Then must I knock, or call when just in sight?
    They will not keep you waiting at that door.

Shall I find comfort, travel-sore and weak?
    Of labour you shall find the sum.
Will there be beds for me and all who seek?
    Yea, beds for all who come.

Christina Rossetti

I never saw a moor,
I never saw the sea;
Yet know I how the heather looks,
And what a wave must be.

I never spoke with God,
Nor visited in heaven;
Yet certain am I of the spot
As if the chart were given.

Emily Dickinson

Break, Break, Break

Break, break, break,
   On thy cold gray stones, O Sea!
And I would that my tongue could utter
   The thoughts that arise in me.

O, well for the fisherman's boy,
   That he shouts with his sister at play!
O, well for the sailor lad,
   That he sings in his boat on the bay!

And the stately ships go on
   To their haven under the hill;
But O for the touch of a vanish'd hand,
   And the sound of a voice that is still!

Break, break, break,
   At the foot of thy crags, O Sea!
But the tender grace of a day that is dead
   Will never come back to me.

Alfred, Lord Tennyson

Elegy — a lyric poem
mourning someone's death.

In the Garden

"When I die
I'll grow wings
And fly.
    Don't grin."

said the caterpillar
crawling by.

Alden Nowlan

"There's poetry all over the place."

Robert Lowell

Light Verse—some poems just aim to delight, to entertain, to have fun with some words.

"Delight is the chief, if not the only, end of poetry."

John Dryden

"Poetry is not a thing said but a way of saying it."

A. E. Housman

"Many wearing rapiers are afraid of goosequills."

William Shakespeare in *Hamlet*

"No surprise for the writer, no surprise for the reader. For me the initial delight is in the surprise of remembering something I didn't know I knew."

Robert Frost

The Launching

Any big event must have
the Ceremony of the Officials.

I had my officials picked out
long before starting to build
my master space rocket.
They included cabinet ministers,
arms makers, generals,
all the boys on the real inside.

When the Big Day came
they stood on a platform
at the foot of the monster
and made speeches
one after the other.

I let them talk
as long as they wanted to,
then, when the last one had finished,
I pushed back a little door
in the side of my brain-child
and invited them to enter.

When the last one had disappeared inside,
I closed the door, walked very deliberately
across to the control panel
and pushed a button.

Imagine my surprise
when it worked.

Raymond Souster

Deus ex machina — "God out of a machine";
the author uses some improbable event to
solve the problems in a story. In ancient
Greek drama, an actor playing one of the
gods would be lowered on stage from above.

equal opportunity

in early canada
when railways were highways

each stop brought new opportunities

there was a rule

    the chinese could only ride
    the last two cars
    of the trains

that is

    until a train derailed
10   killing all those
    in front

(the chinese erected an altar and thanked buddha)

a new rule was made

    the chinese must ride
    the front two cars
    of the trains

that is

    until another accident
    claimed everyone
20   in the back

(the chinese erected an altar and thanked buddha)

after much debate
common sense prevailed

the chinese are now allowed
to sit anywhere
on any train

Jim Wong-Chu

Sir Smasham Uppe

Good afternoon, Sir Smasham Uppe!
We're having tea: do take a cup!
Sugar and milk? Now let me see—
Two lumps, I think? … Good gracious me!
The silly thing slipped off your knee!
Pray don't apologize, old chap:
A very trivial mishap!
So clumsy of you? How absurd!
My dear Sir Smasham, not a word!
10   Now do sit down and have another,
And tell us all about your brother—
You know, the one who broke his head.
Is the poor fellow still in bed?—
A chair—allow me, sir! … Great Scott!
That was a nasty smash! Eh, what?
Oh, not at all: the chair was old—
Queen Anne, or so we have been told.
We've got at least a dozen more:
Just leave the pieces on the floor.
20   I want you to admire our view:
Come nearer to the window, do;
And look how beautiful … Tut, tut!
You didn't see that it was shut?
I hope you are not badly cut!
Not hurt? A fortunate escape!
Amazing! Not a single scrape!
And now, if you have finished tea,
I fancy you might like to see
A little thing or two I've got.
30   That china plate? Yes, worth a lot:
A beauty too … Ah, there it goes!
I trust it didn't hurt your toes?
Your elbow brushed it off the shelf?
Of course: I've done the same myself.
And now, my dear Sir Smasham—oh,
You surely don't intend to go?
You *must* be off? Well, come again.
So glad you're fond of porcelain!

Emile Victor Rieu

An Elegy on the Death of a Mad Dog

Good people all, of every sort,
    Give ear unto my song;
And if you find it wondrous short,
    It cannot hold you long.

In Islington there was a man,
    Of whom the world might say,
That still a godly race he ran
    When'er he went to pray.

A kind and gentle heart he had,
    To comfort friends and foes;
The naked every day he clad,
    When he put on his clothes.

And in that town a dog was found,
    As many dogs there be,
Both mongrel, puppy, whelp, and hound,
    And curs of low degree.

This dog and man at first were friends;
    But when a pique began,
The dog, to gain his private ends,
    Went mad, and bit the man.

Around from all the neighbouring streets
    The wondering neighbours ran,
And swore the dog had lost his wits,
    To bite so good a man.

The wound it seemed both sore and sad
    To every Christian eye:
And while they swore the dog was mad,
    They swore the man would die.

But soon a wonder came to light,
    That showed the rogues they lied;
The man recovered of the bite,
    The dog it was that died.

Oliver Goldsmith

January

OOOOOOOOoooooooo
everyone in this house is sick
everyone   all the furniture
is depressed   even the clever
armchair so recently recovered

we must we must
do something about these walls
they are so weary of it all,
the piano's unfit
and those varnished beasts gathered
in the diningroom are suicidal,
little wonder, and the carpets are chronic

only the dishwasher is really
well   the machinery
of its blue waterfalls
cheerful as ever
its pure cycles admonish us
we hate it

Carol Shields

Highest Standard of Living Yet

"Three-car families" predicted
at Chamber of Commerce meeting.

One for the Master
And one for his Mate
And one for the Monster
To pick up his Date.

Bumper to bumper,
Morning till night,
Three times as many cars
Grounded in flight.

Marya Mannes

The Abundant Life

There's a factory by the side of the river
busily turning out things-things-things,
and it has goods to produce and deliver
regardless of what the future brings.

So the fish must die and the lake grow fetid,
rimmed by a forest where no bird sings,
and as everyone says, it's to be regretted
but who'd want to do without things-things-things?

Bonnie Day

Television

The couch cushions the fall of
Him. A throne of
His. Ah, a time for rest.

Click…Fizz Fizz Fizz.

–first down and goal for…
click
–strike two called…
click
–gunman shoots down many…
click
–and now War and Remembrance

Ah, leans back to relax,
to remember.

–but first a word from our sponsor

Click…Fizz Fizz Fizz.

Hmm, gets up stretches
What was that
I was going
to do?

Robert Wyrwicz

About Being a Member of Our Armed Forces

Remember the early days of the phony war
when men were zombies and women were CWACs
and they used wooden rifles on the firing range?
Well I was the sort of soldier you couldn't trust
with a wooden rifle
and when they gave me a wooden bayonet
life was fraught with peril for my brave comrades
including the sergeant-instructor
I wasn't exactly a soldier tho
10   only a humble airman
who kept getting demoted
                and demoted
                      and demoted
to the point where I finally saluted civilians
And when they trustingly gave me a Sten gun
Vancouver should have trembled in its sleep
for after I fired a whole clip of bullets
at some wild ducks under Burrard Bridge
(on guard duty at midnight)
20   they didn't fly away for five minutes
trying to decide if there was any danger
Not that the war was funny
I took it and myself quite seriously
the way a squirrel in a treadmill does
too close to tears for tragedy
too far from the banana peel for laughter
and I didn't blame anyone for being there
that wars happened wasn't anybody's fault then
now I think it is

Al Purdy

Satire — literature exposing the weaknesses
and follies of a person, institution, belief.

God Bless General Motors Whoever He Is

My brother
is in Labrador
selling cars.
Can you picture it?
In Labrador.
Labrador, land of the Inuit.
The land God gave to Cain.
Land of rivers
and mountains and caribou.
Land of ice and snow
and endless wilderness.
Land untamed, unconquered,
uninhabitable.
As vast as a continent.
Labrador, the final frontier.
And my brother there
selling cars.

And doing well.

Al Pittman

Next to of course god

"next to of course god america i
love you land of the pilgrims' and so forth oh
say can you see by the dawn's early my
country 'tis of centuries come and go
and are no more what of it we should worry
in every language even deafanddumb
thy sons acclaim your glorious name by gorry
by jingo by gee by gosh by gum
why talk of beauty what could be more beautiful than these heroic happy dead
who rushed like lions to the roaring slaughter
they did not stop to think they died instead
then shall the voice of liberty be mute?"

He spoke. And drank rapidly a glass of water

e. e. cummings

the lesson of the moth

i was talking to a moth
the other evening
he was trying to break into
an electric light bulb
and fry himself on the wires

why do you fellows
pull this stunt i asked him
because it is the conventional
thing for moths or why
10   if that had been an uncovered
candle instead of an electric
light bulb you would
now be a small unsightly cinder
have you no sense

plenty of it he answered
but at times we get tired
of using it
we get bored with the routine
and crave beauty
20   and excitement
fire is beautiful
and we know that if we get
too close it will kill us
but what does that matter
it is better to be happy
for a moment
and be burned up with beauty
than to live a long time
and be bored all the while
30   so we wad all our life up
into one little roll
and then we shoot the roll
that is what life is for
it is better to be a part of beauty
for one instant and then cease to
exist than to exist forever

and never be a part of beauty
our attitude toward life
is come easy go easy
40   we are like human beings
used to be before they became
too civilized to enjoy themselves

and before i could argue him
out of his philosophy
he went and immolated himself
on a patent cigar lighter
i do not agree with him
myself i would rather have
half the happiness and twice
50   the longevity

archy — the cockroach
who typed his poems
using Don Marquis's
typewriter.

but at the same time i wish
there was something i wanted
as badly as he wanted to fry himself
                   archy

Don Marquis

he Bat

By day the bat is cousin to the mouse.
He likes the attic of an aging house.

His fingers make a hat about his head.
His pulse beat is so slow we think him dead.

He loops in crazy figures half the night
Among the trees that face the corner light.

But when he brushes up against a screen,
We are afraid of what our eyes have seen:

For something is amiss or out of place
When mice with wings can wear a human face.

Theodore Roethke

aiter! there's an alligator in my coffee

Waiter!...there's an alligator in my coffee.
Are you trying to be funny?
he said:
what do you want for a dime...?
...a circus?
but sir! I said,
he's swimming
around
and around
10   in my coffee
and he might
jump out on the table...
Feed him a lump of sugar! he snarled—
no!...make it two;
it'll weigh him down
and he'll drown.

I dropped two blocks of sugar
into the swamp,
two grist jaws snapped them up
20   and the critter—
he never drowned.
Waiter!...there's an alligator in my coffee.
Kill him! Kill him!
he said:
BASH HIS BRAINS OUT
WITH YOUR SPOON...!
By this time
considerable attention had been drawn:
around my coffee
30   the waiters, the owner,
and customers gathered.

What seems to be the trouble?
the owner inquired,
and I replied:
There's an alligator in my coffee!

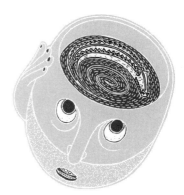

...But the coffee's fresh, he said
and raised the cup to his nose...
Careful! I said,
he'll bite it
40 off
and he replied:
How absurd,
and lowered the cup
level to his mouth and
swallowed
the evidence.

Joe Rosenblatt

Please Do Not Feed the Seals

If you've ever been to the Calgary Zoo
you might have seen
on the wall by the seal tank
a display case filled with
103 pennies, nickels, and dimes,
several pieces of bent wire,
and other small oddities.

You look closer
and read the text:
"This collection was found
in the stomach of a seal
that died at the zoo."

That's not all though,
the coins shown were not the originals.
For those had been stolen
a few days after the display
was first put up.

Jacob Wickland

gainst Broccoli

The local groceries are all out of broccoli,
Loccoli.

Roy Blount, Jr.

he Eel

I don't mind eels
Except as meals.
And the way they feels.

Ogden Nash

ike O'Day

This is the grave of Mike O'Day
Who died maintaining his right of way.
His right was clear, his will was strong,
But he's just as dead as if he'd been wrong.

Anonymous

There was a young lady of Spain
Who was dreadfully sick in a train,
     Not once, but again
     And again and again,
And again and again and again.

Anonymous

he Panther

The panther is like a leopard,
Except it hasn't been peppered.
Should you behold a panther crouch,
Prepare to say Ouch.
Or better yet, if called by a panther,
Don't anther.

Ogden Nash

Dave Morice

Here is Tennyson's famous poem "The Eagle" in its usual form:

He clasps the crag with crooked hands;
Close to the sun in lonely lands,
Ringed with the azure world, he stands.

The wrinkled sea beneath him crawls;
He watches from his mountain walls,
And like a thunderbolt he falls.

help i've just been run over by a bus

having a relationship
    with you
is like riding
    a 3-speed bicycle
in rush-hour traffic
    up yonge st.—

too many people
    altogether
and besides
    it's dangerous—

i got hit
    by a bus 1 day
& didn't know what hit me
till i struck the pavement
& saw this great big
            bus's body
going past me
    2 inches from
                my hand on the ground

what happened
    a man asked
did your bike
    get caught
in the grating?

no i said
            grating, my foot!
a bus just hit me
    what does it look like?

(realizing i could've been killed
   & no one would've
      even noticed
   —not even the bus—
falling in love with you
   was like
being hit
      by a bus—
i wasn't killed
   but I wouldn't do it again.

Gwen Hauser

rue Love

Walking barefoot along the ocean
picnics on a green hillside,
why don't we do these things?
Granted we have gazed at stars
from an empty bus
on eighth street.

Dawn Tweedie

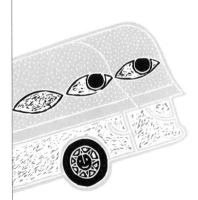

Some poems are street-wise.

The Top Hat

Whether it's just a gag or the old geezer's
a bit queer in the head, it's still refreshing
to see someone walking up Bay Street
with toes out of shoes, patched trousers, frayed suit-coat,
and on his head the biggest, shiniest top hat
since Abe Lincoln,

and walking as if the whole
damn street belonged to him:

which at this moment for my money
it does.

Raymond Souster

The Attack

Only last night Pat was attacked
By three young punks. He was going
By the cemetery when they jumped him,
Dragged him inside behind some tombstones
And beat him up good. "For a while," he told me,
"I thought they might even kill me, and I remember thinking
What a hell of a place to be found dead in."

Raymond Souster

"Poetry is an arrow that cuts through the mind and into the heart."

Greg Marshall

Poetry frequently deals with the big questions of death and love and loneliness. Poetry does not exist in a vacuum. It is the very stuff of life and often life's darker moments are the focus of the poet's attention.

"Poetry is the language of a state of crisis."

Stephane Malarmé

"The only cause for pessimism would be if men and women ceased to write poetry, and they don't."

Elizabeth Drew

Dream 1: The Bush Garden

I stood once more in that garden
sold, deserted and
gone to seed

In the dream I could
see down through the earth, could see
the potatoes curled
like pale grubs in the soil
the radishes thrusting down
their fleshy snouts, the beets
pulsing like slow amphibian hearts

Around my feet
the strawberries were surging, huge
and shining

When I bent
to pick, my hands
came away red and wet

In the dream I said
I should have known
anything planted here
would come up blood

Margaret Atwood

Imagery — using words to stim-
ulate the imagination to see, hear,
taste, touch, smell. Poetry appeals
to the senses.

Sea Lullaby

The old moon is tarnished
With smoke of the flood,
The dead leaves are varnished
With colour like blood,

A treacherous smiler
With teeth white as milk,
A savage beguiler
In sheathings of silk,

The sea creeps to pillage,
She leaps on her prey;
A child of the village
Was murdered today.

She came up to meet him
In a smooth golden cloak,
She choked him and beat him
To death, for a joke.

Her bright locks were tangled,
She shouted for joy,
With one hand she strangled
A strong little boy.

Now in silence she lingers
Beside him all night
To wash her long fingers
In silvery light.

Elinor Wylie

Rumours of War

In my very early years
I must have heard
ominous news broadcasts
on the radio;
they must have mentioned
the Black Forest

for I dreamed a black forest
moving across a map,
I and my rag doll
caught on the coast edge
of the country
I was too young
even to name

Austria Poland Hungary
would have meant nothing
to me
but the Black Forest
came right up our ravine
down over the mountains

and Raggedy Ann
and I woke screaming
out of the clutch of
evil trees

Pat Lowther

Dreamers

Soldiers are citizens of death's grey land,
  Drawing no dividend from time's to-morrows.
In the great hour of destiny they stand,
  Each with his feuds, and jealousies, and sorrows.
Soldiers are sworn to action; they must win
  Some flaming, fatal climax with their lives.
Soldiers are dreamers; when the guns begin,
  They think of firelit homes, clean beds, and wives.
I see them in foul dug-outs, gnawed by rats,
  And in the ruined trenches, lashed with rain.
Dreaming of things they did with balls and bats,
  And mocked by hopeless longing to regain
Bank holidays, and picture shows, and spats,
  And going to the office in the train.

Siegfried Sassoon

104

The Man He Killed

"Had he and I but met
By some old ancient inn,
We should have sat us down to wet
Right many a nipperkin!

"But ranged as infantry,
And staring face to face,
I shot at him as he at me,
And killed him in his place.

"I shot him dead because—
Because he was my foe,
Just so: my foe of course he was;
That's clear enough; although

"He thought he'd 'list, perhaps,
Off-hand-like—just as I—
Was out of work—had sold his traps—
No other reason why.

"Yes, quaint and curious war is!
You shoot a fellow down
You'd treat, if met where any bar is,
Or help to half-a-crown."

Thomas Hardy

"Rumours of War" World War II (1939-1945)

"Dreamers" World War I (1914-1918)

"The Man He Killed" Boer War (1899-1902)

Disabled

He sat in a wheeled chair, waiting for dark,
And shivered in his ghastly suit of grey,
Legless, sewn short at elbow. Through the park
Voices of boys rang saddening like a hymn,
Voices of play and pleasure after day,
Till gathering sleep had mothered them from him.

About this time Town used to swing so gay
When glow-lamps budded in the light-blue trees
And girls glanced lovelier as the air grew dim,
—In the old times, before he threw away his knees.
Now he will never feel again how slim
Girls' waists are, or how warm their subtle hands,
All of them touch him like some queer disease.

There was an artist silly for his face,
For it was younger than his youth, last year.
Now he is old; his back will never brace;
He's lost his colour very far from here,
Poured it down shell-holes till the veins ran dry,
And half his lifetime lapsed in the hot race,
And leap of purple spurted from his thigh.
One time he liked a bloodsmear down his leg,
After the matches carried shoulder-high.

It was after football, when he'd drunk a peg,
He thought he'd better join. He wonders why...
Someone had said he'd look a god in kilts.

That's why; and maybe, too, to please his Meg,
Aye, that was it, to please the giddy jilts,
He asked to join. He didn't have to beg;
Smiling they wrote his lie; aged nineteen years.
Germans he scarcely thought of; and no fears
Of Fear came yet. He thought of jewelled hilts
For daggers in plaid socks; of smart salutes;
And care of arms; and leave; and pay arrears;
Esprit de corps; and hints for young recruits.
And soon, he was drafted out with drums and cheers.

Some cheered him home, but not as crowds cheer Goal.
Only a solemn man who brought him fruits
Thanked him; and then inquired about his soul.
Now, he will spend a few sick years in Institutes,
And do what things the rules consider wise,
And take whatever pity they may dole.
To-night he noticed how the women's eyes
Passed from him to the strong men that were whole.
How cold and late it is! Why don't they come
And put him into bed? Why don't they come?

Wilfred Owen

What the Defence-Plant Worker Said

Bombs have no function except to kill
and making bomb-parts is what I do,
but I have a grocery-cart to fill
and expenses to meet, just the same as you.
The Chamber of Commerce understands.
War-contracts help the economy:
make jobs for hundreds of factory-hands
and add quite a lot to the GNP.

I'd rather make ploughs if I had my way,
but in case of a permanent bombing truce
this plant would shut down and I'd miss my pay.
I can't control what my hands produce.
I wouldn't kill children at play: not me.
I'd never do murder with my own hands
but I'm only a war-plant employee
and the ones getting killed are in foreign lands.

I don't have to see them or hear their cries—
a burnt child's scream or a mother's sob.
Their mangled bodies or blinded eyes
are none of my business. I need my job.
The reason they're killed is to set them free,
but they aren't grateful, so what's the use?
You understand how it is with me—
I can't control what my hands produce.

Bonnie Day

107

Unspoken Hostility

Another lonely bus ride home.
I grab a seat,
and stare out at winter,
then at the floor,
and see four black jube jubes.
Squished,
by an irritated stamp.

A woman gets on,
and scans the bus.
Her eyes skim
past the empty seat beside me,
and flicker back,
uncertain.
She steps towards me,
and sits down.
Uncovering her gloved hands
and placing them on her lap.

Hers,
pale as the cold bitter winter.
While mine,
the earthy tones of spring.

I feel the light contact of her bulky jacket against my own.
The bus swerves,
unexpected.
She is pushed against me.
She jerks,
and straightens her posture.
Her body straight and rigid.
Eyes hard,
putting an empty space between us.

Marites Carino

Nazis

Nazis, the whispers began,
Nazis, when they gathered
and poured over each other
memory of the Old Country
to wash away the dust
of the cold Canadian fields.
Nazis, the voices said
to their backs in the town,
Nazis, to their children
bewildered at school,
Nazis, until they kept alien
to their farms and afraid.

Such relief for us all,
the end of the war,
the enemy now redefined:
the stooped Ukrainians
pausing over their plows.
Communists, we said.
Communists.

Leona Gom

Slice-of-life — an anecdotal sketch of life just as it is, without adornment or exaggeration.

Incident

Once riding in old Baltimore,
Heart-filled, head-filled with glee,
I saw a Baltimorean
Keep looking straight at me.

Now I was eight and very small,
and he was no whit bigger,
And so I smiled, but he poked out
His tongue, and called me, "Nigger."

I saw the whole of Baltimore
From May until December;
Of all the things that happened there
That's all that I remember.

Countee Cullen

Photographs

Belly distends
covers atrophying
organs

on one skeletal leg
a bracelet
placed lovingly

large brown eyes
too big for the head
centre me

in this room
we fuss with hair
flip lazily through magazines

admire sleek models

Alice VanWart

the little purple man

dropped in a drink just for fun
the little purple man sinks right to the bottom
he climbs the ladder into her head
a scream is heard and now she is dead.

Lucy doesn't remember a thing any more,
skies that turned black, passing through doors
doors that lead to who knows where
and they said it was just for fun.

Michael Gossier

Late Night News

The Apocalyptic horsemen
galloped steadily tonight across the screen,
and item after item
prophesied the end of food, of fuel,
of peace, of air, of earth, of us.

"Thank God we don't have kids," you said,
turning off the set.
And I, like all the world out there,
watched my microcosmic square of light
contracting to a pinpoint, disappear.
And I, like all the world out there,
sat alone inside a blackened room,
seeing in the after-image
one final cryptic signature
conclude the document of human history.

Richard Cory

Leona Gom

Whenever Richard Cory went down town,
  We people on the pavement looked at him:
He was a gentleman from sole to crown,
  Clean favoured, and imperially slim.

And he was always quietly arrayed,
  And he was always human when he talked;
But still he fluttered pulses when he said,
  "Good-morning," and he glittered when he walked.

And he was rich—yes, richer than a king—
  And admirably schooled in every grace:
In fine, we thought that he was everything
  To make us wish that we were in his place.

So on we worked, and waited for the light,
  And went without the meat, and cursed the bread;
And Richard Cory, one calm summer night,
  Went home and put a bullet through his head.

Edwin Arlington Robinson

Carved

Two small dogs stood by a dead black bird
And the black bird was very dead.

The two dogs stood by the bird like large lions
But they never touched the dead thing, once.

They would like to have eaten the black thing
But it was very dead with red ants

Sawing its neck away like stone masons
And the red ants were very much alive.

So all the time the dogs stood they barked there
Because they couldn't eat the black thing.

Something large about that black bird.
It was being eaten by red death

While the two large-lion small dogs just stood,
Barking: they never touched the black thing,

And the black thing never looked at them, once.
It was indifferent to two small dogs.

Maybe it did not hear those large lions
Or maybe the black bird felt sorry for the small dogs.

Meanwhile the dead went on being dead and the living
     living.

Jon Silkin

> "Poetry therefore is an art of imitation…a representing, counterfeiting, or figuring forth: to speak metaphorically, a speaking picture."
>
> **Sir Philip Sidney in *A Defence of Poetry* (1580)**

A poem has a video component as well as an audio component. It speaks to the eye and to the ear.

Audio—from the Latin, "I hear"

Video—from the Latin, "I see"

Charlottetown Harbour

An old docker with gutted cheeks,
time arrested in the used-up-knuckled hands
crossed on his lap, sits
in a spell of the glinting water.

He dreams of times in the cider sunlight
when masts stood up like stubble;
but now a gull cries, lights,
flounces its wings ornately, folds them,
and the waves slop among the weed-grown piles.

Milton Acorn

Saturday Night

Every five minutes they turn,
with their tires like sirens,
tusking the dirt up on the creek road,
and drive back through town—

> slowing down on Main Street, manoeuvring
> between the farmers' cars, hooting
> at girls on the pavement who reply
> with little hen movements, laughing, waiting.

The boys sport leather jackets and levis;
but that's their underwear,
the car is their real clothing:
at Taylor's Corner they turn again,
their Hollywood mufflers
making sounds furious, derisive, vulgar—
like a bear growling and breaking wind,

> and roar through Main Street again.

Alden Nowlan

Cargoes

Quinquereme of Nineveh from distant Ophir,
Rowing home to haven in sunny Palestine,
With a cargo of ivory,
And apes and peacocks,
Sandalwood, cedarwood, and sweet white wine.

Stately Spanish galleon coming from the Isthmus,
Dipping through the Tropics by the palm-green shores,
With a cargo of diamonds,
Emeralds, amethysts,
Topazes, and cinnamon, and gold moidores.

Dirty British coaster with a salt-caked smoke-stack,
Butting through the Channel in the mad March days,
With a cargo of Tyne coal,
Road-rails, pig-lead,
Firewood, iron-ware, and cheap tin trays.

John Masefield

Sea-Fever

I must down to the seas again, to the lonely sea and the sky,
And all I ask is a tall ship and a star to steer her by,
And the wheel's kick and the wind's song and the white sail's
    shaking
And a grey mist on the sea's face and a grey dawn breaking.

I must down to the seas again, for the call of the running tide
Is a wild call and a clear call that may not be denied;
And all I ask is a windy day with the white clouds flying,
And the flung spray and the blown spume, and the sea-gulls
    crying.

I must down to the seas again to the vagrant gypsy life.
To the gull's way and the whale's way where the wind's like a
    whetted knife;
And all I ask is a merry yarn from a laughing fellow-rover,
And quiet sleep and a sweet dream when the long trick's over.

John Masefield

The Song My Paddle Sings

West wind blow from your prairie nest,
Blow from the mountains, blow from the west.
The sail is idle, the sailor too;
O! wind of the west, we wait for you.
Blow, blow!
I have wooed you so,
But never a favour you bestow.
You rock your cradle the hills between,
But scorn to notice my white lateen.

I stow the sail, unship the mast:
I wooed you long but my wooing's past;
My paddle will lull you into rest.
O! drowsy wind of the drowsy west,
Sleep, sleep,
By your mountain steep,
Or down where the prairie grasses sweep!
Now fold in slumber your laggard wings,
For soft is the song my paddle sings.

August is laughing across the sky,
Laughing while paddle, canoe and I,
Drift, drift,
Where the hills uplift
On either side of the current swift.

The river rolls in its rocky bed;
My paddle is plying its way ahead;
Dip, dip,
While the waters flip
In foam as over their breast we slip.

And oh, the river runs swifter now;
The eddies circle about my bow.
Swirl, swirl!
How the ripples curl
In many a dangerous pool awhirl!

And forward far the rapids roar,
Fretting their margin for evermore.
Dash, dash,
With a mighty crash,
They seethe, and boil, and bound, and splash!

Be strong, O paddle! be brave, canoe!
The reckless waves you must plunge into.
Reel, reel,
On your trembling keel,
But never a fear my craft will feel.

We've raced the rapid, we're far ahead!
The river slips through its silent bed.
Sway, sway,
As the bubbles spray
And fall in tinkling tunes away.

And up on the hills against the sky,
A fir tree rocking its lullaby,
Swings, swings,
Its emerald wings,
Swelling the song that my paddle sings.

E. Pauline Johnson

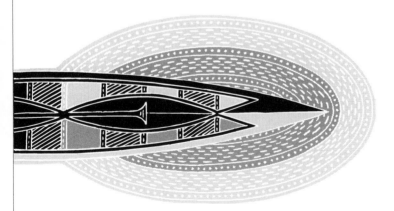

The Lonely Land

Cedar and jagged fir
uplift sharp barbs
against the gray
and cloud-piled sky;
and in the bay
blown spume and windrift
and thin, bitter spray
snap
at the whirling sky;
and the pine trees
lean one way.

A wild duck calls
to her mate,
and the ragged
and passionate tones
stagger and fall,
and recover,
and stagger and fall,
on these stones—
are lost
in the lapping of water
on smooth, flat stones.

This is a beauty
of dissonance,
this resonance
of stony strand,
this smoky cry
curled over a black pine
like a broken
and wind-battered branch

when the wind
bends the tops of the pines
and curdles the sky
from the north.

This is the beauty
of strength
broken by strength
and still strong.

A. J. M. *Smith*

Life in the City

Noon clouds, sunny-side up
    On the skillet of the atmosphere,
  Ashtrays for the smokestacks.

The rooftops sleep under blankets of snow,
  While the city towers
    Are a bitter scurry of activity.

The telephone poles hold hands across the city,
  And the fire hydrants sit and
    Count the passing cars.

Empty parking lots are deserts of snow
  Ending at streets worn to their bone
    Of asphalt under the melted layer of white skin.

The skeletons of trees line the streets,
      Still standing
  In their wood and metal boxes,
    Once visibly filled with earth, by the roadside.

Parked cars betray their age by their coat
      Of white fluff,
    While the parking meters shiver, thin and naked
      On the sidewalk.

The sun burns red as it cuts the horizon
    Of boxes and curves, ending another
  Winter afternoon in the city.

Christian Bouchard

Picturesque — The language of poetry is the
language of pictures. Poetry is a picture-making
factory creating scenes for the imagination.

The Singer

Crackle and flash almost in the kitchen sink—the
thunderclap follows even as I
jump back frightened,
afraid to touch metal—

> The roofgutters pouring down
> whole rivers, making holes in the earth—
> The electric bulbs fade and go out,
> another thin crackling lights the window
> and in the instant before the next onslaught of kettledrums,

a small bird, I don't know its name,
among the seagreen tossed leaves
> begins its song.

Denise Levertov

Lyric — A lyric is a
short poem expressing
a personal feeling or
attitude about some
topic.

The Grey Squirrel

Like a small grey
coffeepot
sits the squirrel.
He is not,

all he should be,
kills by dozens
trees, and eats
his red-brown cousins.

The keeper, on the
other hand
, who shot him, is
a Christian, and

loves his enemies,
which shows
the squirrel was not
one of those.

Humbert Wolfe

Changes

As you came with me in silence
to the pump in the long grass

I heard much that you could not hear:
the bite of the spade that sank it,

the slithering and grumble
as the mason mixed his mortar,

and women coming with white buckets
like flashes on their ruffled wings.

The cast-iron rims of the lid
clinked as I uncovered it,

something stirred in its mouth.
I had a bird's eye view of a bird,

finch-green, speckly white,
nesting on dry leaves, flattened, still,

suffering the light.
So I roofed the citadel

as gently as I could, and told you
and you gently unroofed it

but where was the bird now?
There was a single egg, pebbly white,

and in the rusted bend of the spout
tail feathers splayed and sat tight.

So tender, I said, "Remember this.
It will be good for you to retrace this path

when you have grown away and stand at last
at the very centre of the empty city."

Seamus Heaney

The Bull Calf

The thing could barely stand. Yet taken
from his mother and the barn smells
he still impressed with his pride,
with the promise of sovereignty in the way
his head moved to take us in.
The fierce sunlight tugging the maize from the ground
licked at his shapely flanks.
He was too young for all that pride.
I thought of the deposed Richard II.

10   "No money in bull calves," Freeman had said.
The visiting clergyman rubbed the nostrils
now snuffing pathetically at the windless day.
"A pity," he sighed.
My gaze slipped off his hat toward the empty sky
that circled over the black knot of men,
over us and the calf waiting for the first blow.

Struck,
the bull calf drew in his thin forelegs
as if gathering strength for a mad rush…
20   tottered…raised his darkening eyes to us,
and I saw we were at the far end
of his frightened look, growing smaller and smaller
till we were only the ponderous mallet
that flicked his bleeding ear
and pushed him over on his side, stiffly,
like a block of wood.

Below the hill's crest
the river snuffled on the improvised beach.
We dug a deep pit and threw the dead calf into it.
30   It made a wet sound, a sepulchral gurgle,
as the warm sides bulged and flattened.
Settled, the bull calf lay as if asleep,
one foreleg over the other,
bereft of pride and so beautiful now,
without movement, perfectly still in the cool pit,
I turned away and wept.

Irving Layton

The Shark

He seemed to know the harbour,
So leisurely he swam;
His fin,
Like a piece of sheet-iron
Three-cornered,
And with knife-edge,
Stirred not a bubble
As it moved
With its base-line on the water.

His body was tubular
And tapered
And smoke-blue,
And as he passed the wharf
He turned,
And snapped at a flat-fish
That was dead and floating.
And I saw the flash of a white throat,
And a double row of white teeth,
And eyes of metallic grey,
Hard and narrow and slit.

Then out of the harbour,
With that three-cornered fin
Shearing without a bubble the water
Lithely,
Leisurely,
He swam—
That strange fish,
Tubular, tapered, smoke-blue,
Part vulture, part wolf,
Part neither—for his blood was cold.

E. J. Pratt

```
the
      sky
            was
can   dy    lu
minous
            edible
spry
      pinks shy
lemons
greens   coo 1 choc
o l a t e
s .

   un    der,
   a     lo
c o
mo
      tive      s  pout
                     ing
                        vi
                        o
                        lets
```

e. e. cummings

ho Has Seen the Wind?

Who has seen the wind?
  Neither I nor you;
But when the leaves hang trembling
  The wind is passing thro'.

Who has seen the wind?
  Neither you nor I;
But when the trees bow down their heads
  The wind is passing by.

Christina Rossetti

Spring is like a perhaps hand
(which comes carefully
out of Nowhere)arranging
a window,into which people look(while
people stare
arranging and changing placing
carefully there a strange
thing and a known thing here)and

changing everything carefully

spring is like a perhaps
Hand in a window
(carefully to
and fro moving New and
Old things,while
people stare carefully
moving a perhaps
fraction of flower here placing
an inch of air there)and

without breaking anything.

e. e. cummings

Nothing Gold Can Stay

Nature's first green is gold,
Her hardest hue to hold.
Her early leaf's a flower;
But only so an hour.
Then leaf subsides to leaf.
So Eden sank to grief,
So dawn goes down to day.
Nothing gold can stay.

Robert Frost

Abundance

The moon: hoof-print in ice.

Someone's shoes chewing an icy path.
The wasted intricacy of each snowflake.
A field without a man in it.
A rusted plow filling with snow.

Roo Borson

Mood — the atmosphere
of the poem; the feelings
it suggests.

Mirrors

Mirrors are always magical.
So the child knows
who first sees one: the strange object
in which the other little girl appears
wearing the same dress, encircled in the same arms;
smiles, frowns, looks puzzled, cries, all the same
but somehow different.
For the other child does not have flesh, feels shiny to touch
and cold like the mirror's surface.
Mirrors are magic, and behind their surface
surely there is another Alice world
where you can walk and talk.

Mirrors are solid lakes,
and you could drown
beneath them if their outer layer cracked,
spin down and meet your real self far below,
a mermaid princess combing out your hair
before a magic mirror.

Elizabeth Brewster

The New Bicycle

All the molecules in the house
re-adjust on its arrival,
make way for its shining presence
its bright dials,
and after it has settled
and the light
has explored its surfaces
—and the night—
they compose themselves again
in another order.

One senses the change at once
without knowing what one senses.
Has somebody cleaned the windows
used different soap
or is there a bowl of flowers
on the mantelpiece?—
for the air makes another shape
it is thinner or denser,
a new design
is invisibly stamped upon it.

How we all adapt ourselves
to the bicycle
aglow in the furnace room,
turquoise where turquoise
has never before been seen,
its chrome gleaming
on gears and pedals,
its spokes glistening.
Lightly resting on the incised
rubber of its airy tires
it has changed us all.

P. K. Page

argins XIV

Night
and main street
all around me
lights
making signs to me
reflected
colouring the rain-washed sidewalk
here
I stand
10   against a wall
beneath an awning
waiting for a black-haired girl
to get off duty
from the cafe
across the street
there
she is
coming out the door
glancing up
20   turning up her coat collar
she walks away
and around the corner
gone
in the rain
now coming down harder
spattering
splattering reflections
and lights blurred
and her
30   gone
and I
standing here against a wall
beneath an awning
waiting

Now
just waiting

Red Lane

Dreams

Hold fast to dreams
For if dreams die
Life is a broken-winged bird
That cannot fly.

Hold fast to dreams
For when dreams go
Life is a barren field
Frozen with snow.

Langston Hughes

I will walk with leg muscles

which are strong

as the sinews of the shins of the little caribou calf.

I will walk with leg muscles

which are strong

as the sinews of the shins of the little hare.

I will take care not to go towards the dark.

I will go towards the day.

traditional Inuit song

Haiku

A traditional and modern Japanese art form.

Traditional Japanese haiku contained a "season-word" and rigidly followed a 5-7-5 pattern of 17 syllables.

Modern haiku often stress emotion, bypass the reference to nature, and break the traditional pattern.

Avoid wordiness, be concise.

Encapsulate a scene or emotion in haiku.

A butterfly
in the cold: it flies in pursuit
of its own soul.

Takahama Kyoshi

Like a father
and also like a mother,
the huge summer tree.

Tomiyasu Fusei

I read a book—
somewhere within the book
an insect chirps.

Tomiyasu Fusei

all translated from the Japanese by Makoto Ueda

Heavens

The ferocious stars
keep their distance, become
a conversation piece

D. G. Jones

Field Notes

The wild geese, wavering
fly south; sunlit
the cricket climbs the grey rock

D. G. Jones

Orchard

In the late sunlight, a robin
is the only apple
in the apple leaves

D. G. Jones

The Wind Disturbs

—the wind disturbs
below the waterfall
the harebells
and
wild columbine

D. G. Jones

Sunday

Once driving

fast gravel hitting hard and

spraying past

a small green and white house

bleached wooden fences

peeling paint from a sign pointing

and the hill that up and up

and then the feeling that

everything inside is rushing to the surface

explosion

the lake on the left

a field of raspberries on the right

Sharon Gazeley

The Imagist

"The moon is a slice of canteloupe,
And the stars are the scraped-out seed.
The sky is a deep blue plate," I said.
But my sister replied: "Indeed!"

"The field of vetch is a purple lake,
And the mowing-machine's a yacht.
The silo's a light-house," I pointed out.
But my brother remarked—"So what?"

Bonnie Day

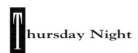

Thursday Night

> "Interpretation is the revenge
> of the intellect upon art."
>
> **Susan Sontag**

The undecided
    shoppers seek neon advice,
        billboard counselling.

Tanya Kanigan

Poetry

People
who analyse poems
    word
      for word
Should be awakened some
    Thursday morning
to the sound of a chainsaw
    cutting through their left leg

I really had no reason
    to pick
      a Thursday
      or a chainsaw
      or a left leg

But someone will
        undoubtedly
think one up.

Richard Lees

The Base Stealer

Poised between going on and back, pulled
Both ways taut like a tightrope-walker,
Fingertips pointing the opposites.
Now bouncing tiptoe like a dropped ball
Or a kid skipping rope, come on, come on,
Running a scattering of steps sidewise,
How he teeters, skitters, tingles, teases,
Taunts them, hovers like an ecstatic bird,
He's only flirting, crowd him, crowd him,
Delicate, delicate, delicate, delicate—now!

Robert Francis

The Rebel

When I
die
I'm sure
I will have a
Big Funeral...
Curiosity
seekers...
coming to see
if I
am really
Dead...
or just
trying to make
Trouble...

Mari Evans

"Art's single greatest potential is—surprise."

Guillaume Apollinaire

P oetry 3000—the poetry of the future. But just maybe the future is already here.

Concrete poetry is experimental poetry. Concrete poetry is the "avant garde" of the poetic community. Attention is placed on the letters, the syllables, the words themselves, the "stuff" out of which the poem is made.

visual—letters, words, and images to see

phonetic—syllables, words, and sounds to hear

kinetic—letters and words that move

Concrete poetry is meant first to be seen, and because of this appeal to the visual and the kinetic, it is able to bridge linguistic barriers. Concrete poetry, like music, dance, film, and painting has the potential to become an international, universal mode of artistic expression.

"He [the poet] unlocks our chains and admits us to a new scene."

Ralph Waldo Emerson

"Poetry is the tip of one's pencil."

Jill Affleck

Calligram — The poem's shape shows what it is about.

Calligram, 15 May 1915

The sky's as blue as ink
My eyes drown in it and sink

Darkness a shell whines over me
I write this under a willow tree

translated from the French by O. Bernard

Guillaume Apollinaire (France)

ranquil Nights

Ryan Rebello (Canada)

Paul de Vree (Belgium)

川 (kawa) = river

州 (sasu) = sand-bank

Seiichi Niikuni (Japan)

ping pong
ping pong ping
pong ping pong
ping pong

Eugen Gomringer (Switzerland)

Cine-poem — a poem designed in the form of the individual frames of a motion picture (cinema = the movies).

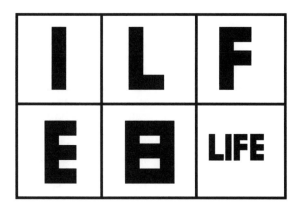

Décio Pignatari (Brazil)

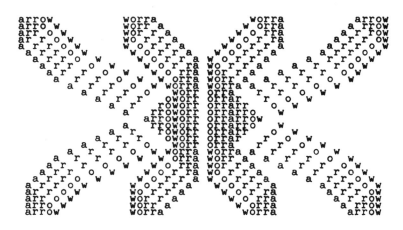

bp Nichol (Canada)

" Turnips are"

turnips are
inturps are
urnspit are
tinspur are
rustpin are
stunrip are
piturns are
ritpuns are
punstir are
nutrips are
suntrip are
untrips are
spinrut are
runspit are
pitnurs are
runtsip are
puntsir are
turnsip are
tipruns are
turpsin are
spurtin

bp Nichol (Canada)

The Computer's First Birthday Card

many returns happy
many turns happier
happy turns remain
happy remains turn
turns remain happy
turn happy remains
remains turn happy
mains return happy
happy mains return
main happy returns
main turns happier
happier main turns
happier many turns
many happier turns
many happier turns
many happier turns
er turns er turns?
happy er er happy?
er error er check!
turn er pre turns!
many happy turners
+ $ - 1 - 0 ½ † • / £ (& ?
many gay whistlers
no no no no no no!
many gainsboroughs
stop stop stop stp
happier constables
01 01 01 01 01 01 01
raise police pay p
ost early for chri
stmas watch forest
fires get well soo
n bon voyage KRRGK
many happy returns
eh? eh? eh? eh? eh?

Edwin Morgan (England)

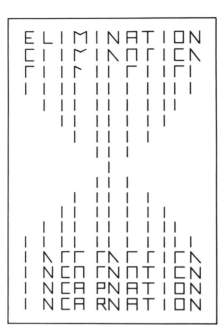

Frans Vanderlinde (Holland)

```
r o s e r o s e r o s               e r o s e
r o s e r o s e r o s e r o s e r o s e
r o s e r o s e r o s e r o s e r o s e
r o s e r o s e r o s e r o s e r o s e
r o s e r o s e r o s e r o s e r o s e
r o s e r o s e r o s e r o s e r o s e
r o s e r o s e r o s e r o s e r o s e
r o s e r o s e r o s e r o s e r o s e
r o s e r o s e r o s e r o s e r o s e
r o s e r o s e r o s e r o s e r o s e
r o s e r o s e r o s e r o s e r o s e
r o s e r o s e r o s e r o s e r o s e
                              e r o s
```

Timm Uhlrichs (Germany)

Eros = the Greek god of love.

Klaus Burkhardt (Germany)

Loch — hole
wenn — when
nichts — nothing
mehr — more
da — there
ist — is
um — around
was — what
drum — therefore

Loch ist loch.

Hole is hole.

reden

schweigen um sich nicht reden zu hören

reden um

schweigen um sich nicht reden zu

reden um sich

schweigen um sich nicht reden

reden um sich nicht

schweigen um sich nicht

reden um sich nicht schweigen

schweigen um sich

reden um sich nicht schweigen zu

schweigen um

reden um sich nicht schweigen zu hören

schweigen

Timm Uhlrichs (Germany)

schweigen (noun) = silence
um (prep) = about, around
sich (pronoun) = oneself, himself
nicht (adverb) = not, no
reden (verb) = to speak, to talk
zu (prep/adverb) = to/too
hören (verb) = to hear, to listen

Read the poem 3 ways:
1. Upright
2. Upside down
3. Sideways

to keep silent in order not to hear oneself speak
to speak in order not to hear oneself keep silent

like attracts like

like   attracts   like

like   attracts   like

like   attracts   like

like   attracts   like

like   attracts   like

like attracts like

like attracts like

likeattractslike

likattractslike

liketradke

liketradke

likeratilse

littelike

Emmett Williams (U.S.A.)

b o i s

b o i s

d o i s

d o i s

d o i s

b o i s

ꝏ o i s

José Line Grünewald (Brazil)

d o i s = two

b o i s = oxen

ꝏ = two yoked oxen

144

 Moonshot Sonnet

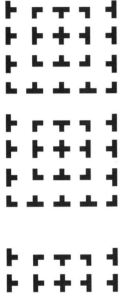

Mary Ellen Solt (U.S.A.)

pó = dust
e = and
mó = millstone

poema
poema
poema
poema
poema
poema
pó
mó

Edgard Braga (Brazil)

July 20, 1969
Astronaut Neil Armstrong becomes the first person from Earth to walk on the moon.

"One small step for man; One giant leap for mankind."

Mary Ellen Solt captures the moment in a Petrarchan sonnet.

A computer poem in six scenes!

Sweethearts

```
s   w   e   e   t   h   e   a   r   t   s
s   w   e   e   t   h   e   a   r   t   s
s   w   e   e   t   h   e   a   r   t   s
s   w   e   e   t   h   e   a   r   t   s
s   w   e   e   t   h   e   a   r   t   s
s   w   e   e   t   h   e   a   r   t   s
s   w   e   e   t   h   e   a   r   t   s
s   w   e   e   t   h   e   a   r   t   s
s   w   e   e   t   h   e   a   r   t   s
s   w   e   e   t   h   e   a   r   t   s
s   w   e   e   t   h   e   a   r   t   s
```

```
                t   h   e
s       e                       a
s       e   e   t   h   e                   s
```

```
                t   h   e
s   w   e   e   t   h   e   a   r   t   s
s       e   e   t   h   e
                            a           s
                t   h   e
s       e                       a
s       e   e   t   h   e                   s
```

```
              t   h   e
s   w   e   e   t   h   e   a   r   t   s
s       e   e
s               t           a   r       s
```

```
                                    s
s

                            a
                t

                                r
                            a       t

s                           a
    e
```

```
              t   h   e
    w                       a   r
s               t           a   r   t   s
```

Emmett Williams (U.S.A.)

"A poem is a small machine made out of words."

William Carlos Williams

"All poetry is experimental poetry."

Wallace Stevens

were indian concepts

The Global Village
The Total Systems
Participatory Democracy
The Tribal Society
Electronic Environment
The Welfare State

4,000 YEARS AGO

Duke Redbird/Marty Dunn (Canada)

unter's Lament

GOOSE

GOOSE

GOOSE

WHY   FLY   SO   HIGH   ?   GOOSE

GOOSE

GOOSE

GOOSE

Edward John (Canada)

THE SOARING SIXTIES

```
          X
          X
          X
          X
          X
          X
```

Paul Donegan (Canada)

Drunk Driver in Concrete

I'M	ALRIGHT	TO	DRIVE!
I'M	ALRIGHT	TA	DRIVE!
I'M	ALRETE	TI	DRIEV?!
I'M	ALREDE	TE	DIVE?
I'M	ALREADY	TO	DIE...

James Dale (Canada)

North American Nutrition

```
F O D
F A S T
 F A S T T
 F A S T T
  F A S T
```

⊽⊏⊡⊐

Sean Jara (Canada)

Golf

THE FRONT NINE

```
F O R E
C H I P
PU TL
F O U R

F I VE
PU TL
PU TL
DR O P
F I VE
```

THE BACK NINE

```
DR ! P
DR O P
CL UB
W A I T

DR O P
DR O P
CL UB
DR O P
NI NE
```

E. J. Barry (Canada)

EXHIBITION

Visual Poems, Non-Syntactic Prose,
Minimal Fiction, Numerical Art, etc.

Also offset posters, books, chapbooks, cards…

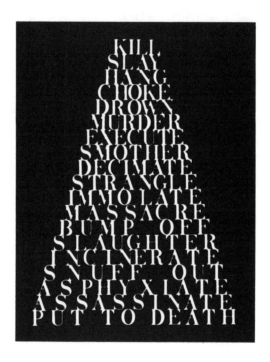

WALK THE EARTH
RESUSCITATE
INVIGORATE
PROPAGATE
ENERGIZE
ACTIVATE
CONTINUE
TURN ON
BREATHE
ANIMATE
SUBSIST
PREVAIL
ENDURE
THRIVE
VIVIFY
ROUSE
ABIDE
EXIST
LIVE

Richard Kostelanetz (U.S.A.)

Write a poem in the Kostelanetz style.

Mount the poem for exhibition.

Stress shape, pattern, symmetry.

 **E**pithalamium II

```
he  = êle
&   = e
she = ela


S = serpens
h = homo
e = eva
```

Pedro Xisto (Brazil)

ZEN

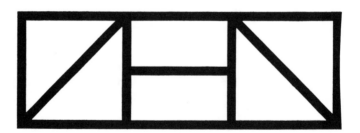

Pedro Xisto (Brazil)

> "Poetry is the exposure of yourself to the cold wind."
>
> **Luanne Martineau**

A poet tells us where we have been and sometimes where we are going. A poet keeps us in touch with who we are.

These poems are about family, and there is nothing more real to most than family or the absence of family.

As we grow older we join the larger family of humanity, but our earliest memories are of close family—of warmth and security, of pain and sometimes disintegration. Family is an excellent starting point when writing poetry. We have all been there and we all relate to the realities of family.

> "The Poet...he can make every word he speaks draw blood."
>
> **Walt Whitman**

> "Poetry is the algebra of the heart."
>
> **e. e. cummings**

> "Home is the place where, when you have to go there,
>
> They have to take you in."
>
> **Robert Frost in**
> **"The Death of the Hired Man"**

First Lesson

The thing to remember about fathers is, they're men.
A girl has to keep it in mind.
They are dragon-seekers, bent on improbable rescues.
Scratch any father, you find
Someone chock-full of qualms and romantic terrors,
Believing change is a threat—
Like your first shoes with heels on, like your first bicycle
It took such months to get.

Walk in strange woods, they warn you about the snakes there.
Climb, and they fear you'll fall.
Books, angular boys, or swimming in deep water—
Fathers mistrust them all.
Men are the worriers. It is difficult for them
To learn what they must learn:
How you have a journey to take and very likely,
For a while, will not return.

Phyllis McGinley

Piano

Softly, in the dusk, a woman is singing to me;
Taking me back down the vista of years, till I see
A child sitting under the piano, in the boom of the tingling strings
And pressing the small, poised feet of a mother who smiles as she sings.

In spite of myself, the insidious mastery of song
Betrays me back, till the heart of me weeps to belong
To the old Sunday evenings at home, with winter outside
And hymns in the cozy parlour, the tinkling piano our guide.

So now it is vain for the singer to burst into clamour
With the great black piano appassionato. The glamour
Of childish days is upon me, my manhood is cast
Down in the flood of remembrance, I weep like a child for the past.

D. H. Lawrence

Long Way Home

All afternoon, my mother
humming daydreams in her kitchen,
cutting up celery and onions,
stuffing the bird,
basting to the schedule
of a gentle oven bell,
only to set the burnt offerings
before an empty chair.

The embarrassed minutes on the phone
while the bartender pages my father.

The long walk down to the club
to fetch him home to a cold supper,
his weight leaning
on my ten-year-old shoulders
like a cross.

Pat Jasper

Strike

My son is trying to
figure out why his
dad has gone from driving to
walking about with a
placard saying more money and
why he
always comes home without any

His dad is trying to
figure out where his
son goes every evening with a
tin cup and his toy monkey and
where the
money on his dresser keeps coming from

And I am trying to
figure out how to
explain the union to the boy and
childhood to the man who
doesn't seem to have had one

Ruth Wilson

The Dancer

I never expected to feel like this
At my age. I thought by this time I'd be
Calm and serene,
Occupied by things like gourmet recipes,
And refinishing old tables.

Instead of that it's like seventeen again,
March flashes through my flesh as it did then
Leaving me weak and warm and wondering
What happens next? Will people think I'm strange
With my hair long and straight, though streaked with grey?

Why can't I reconcile myself to proper dresses
And hairdos more becoming to my age?
My mother did, and lived in peace
Or did she? I'm sure she never felt
As I do now. But how would I know, really?

My daughters think I'm sensible and solid,
Someone who's always there, to call them in the morning,
To cook the roast, and order pants from Eaton's.
What would they say, I wonder, if I told them
I'd like to go play marbles in the mud?

Or waltz around the kitchen while a country singer
Warbles about falling to pieces. Is that what I'm doing?
I never was much of a dancer, although
I always wanted to be. Maybe that
Or something else is what's wrong with me now.

Helen Porter

Follower

My father worked with a horse-plough,
His shoulders globed like a full sail strung
Between the shafts and the furrow.
The horses strained at his clicking tongue.

An expert. He would set the wing
And fit the bright-steel-pointed sock.
The sod rolled over without breaking.
At the headrig, with a single pluck

Of reins, the sweating team turned round
And back into the land. His eye
Narrowed and angled at the ground,
Mapping the furrow exactly.

I stumbled in his hob-nailed wake,
Fell sometimes on the polished sod;
Sometimes he rode me on his back
Dipping and rising to his plod.

I wanted to grow up and plough,
To close one eye, stiffen my arm.
All I ever did was follow
In his broad shadow round the farm.

I was a nuisance, tripping, falling,
Yapping always. But today
It is my father who keeps stumbling
Behind me, and will not go away.

Seamus Heaney

"For whatever embryo the poem starts from — an
event, an emotion, a character, a scene, an insight, an
idea — its theme never exists in isolation."

Elizabeth Drew

Bothering Me at Last

Where is my mother?
Has she gone to the store for food,
or is she in the cellar shovelling coal
into the furnace to keep the house warm?
Or is she on her knees scrubbing the floor?
I thought I saw her in bed
holding a hand to her heart, her mouth open:
"I can't breathe, son. Take me to a hospital."
I looked for her in the cellar.
I looked for her in bed, and found her in her coffin,
bothering me at last.

David Ignatow

my father hurt-
ing at the table
sitting hurting
at suppertime
deep inside very
far down inside
because I can't stand the ginger
in the beef and greens
he cooked for us tonight
and years later tonight
that look on his face
appears now on mine
my children
my food
their food
my father
their father
me mine
the father
very far
very very far
inside

The poet has the ear and eye
of the reporter, with the talent
and sensitivity of the artist-
philosopher.

Fred Wah

otherlove

In one corner of the room
a woman sits
my mother
As a child
beaten
abused

She grew strong
Strong enough to beat me worse
And now I am strong
10   And with my child
I fight inside
to spare the rod

In one corner of the room
a woman sits
my mother
for whom I have felt hate
distrust
The rod with which I was beaten
hardened
20   and became her eyes
and her voice
And now as she smiles
It is still difficult
to remove from my thoughts
the memory of the lash
on my back
and the harshness and cruelty
of the hardness in her voice
and her eyes…

30   Perhaps
it was not possible

Sylvia Parker

Requiem of a War-Baby

I was born in August, 1942—conceived on a Christmas
leave.
I know little of my father, having seen him just once,
when I was three.
The room was dark and a turf fire burned.
I stood on one of the little boxes that clipped to each side
of the fender.

And there were fruit gums and Mummy was happy and
it was very quiet.
I didn't pay much attention to the tall man.
I think I preferred the sweets he had brought.

In the grim school years when it is so crucial to be the
same as everyone else,
There were many flushed moments.
They knew so much more about him than I did.

I remember my last Christmas at the Primary.
It was snowing.
I hit one of the "enemies" with a hard snowball, as she
was running to hide in the toilets.

Someone shouted to her, "Go home and tell your daddy,
cry-baby."
"It's more than Joan Watton can do anyway," was the
swift reply.
The snowball I was holding dropped from my hands.
I remember the hush, and the eyes.
I remember the whiteness, and the blood rising in my
face.

The Head called us from the yard.
He slapped with a whippy cane one each outstretched
frozen right hand.
My turn—"Betty Pedlow insulted me, sir."
I felt not so much the physical pain, but the injustice,
As the cane came down, first on one hand and then the
other.

All through school I told the little fibs—
"Working in England, killed in the war…."
Anything that sounded legitimate.

There was a browned photograph that was kept in a
    handbag on top of the wardrobe.
I would stand on a chair, and gape at the big, crew-cutted
    soldier—
Making myself hate him, because I felt I ought.

It wasn't until I was fifteen that they decided I was old
    enough to know.
"You see, Joan, he sent no money—he asked for a di-
    vorce, and then he wrote and said he had had a child
    to another woman—
And your Mammy had to go out to work and…."
It was stark reality to have to swallow at that dreamy age.

But despite it all I wanted to meet him.
Then I found his letters—weak, weak…
With a tired disgust, my last curiosity thwarted.

It's easy to dramatize.
The absolute truth is, I am not all that much different
    from a daughter with a father.

Joan Watton

aternity

One wept whose only child was dead,
    New-born, ten years ago.
"Weep not; he is in bliss," they said.
    She answered, "Even so.

"Ten years ago was born in pain
    A child, not now forlorn.
But oh, ten years ago, in vain,
    A mother, a mother was born."

Alice Meynell

Night Poem

There is nothing to be afraid of,
it is only the wind
changing to the east, it is only
your father   the thunder
your mother   the rain

In this country of water
with its beige moon damp as a mushroom,
its drowned stumps and long birds
that swim, where the moss grows
on all sides of the trees
and your shadow is not your shadow
but your reflection,

your true parents disappear
when the curtain covers your door.
We are the others,
the ones from under the lake
who stand silently beside your bed
with our heads of darkness.
We have come to cover you
with red wool,
with our tears and distant whispers.

You rock in the rain's arms,
the chilly ark of your sleep,
while we wait, your night
father and mother,
with our cold hands and dead flashlight,
knowing we are only
the wavering shadows thrown
by one candle, in this echo
you will hear twenty years later.

Margaret Atwood

Griffin of the Night

I'm holding my son in my arms
sweating after nightmares
small me
fingers in his mouth
his other fist clenched in my hair
small me
sweating after nightmares

Michael Ondaatje

Family

I followed my father
 And he guided me to knowledge
I followed my mother
 And she showed me good sense
I followed my brother
 And he led me to girls
But when I followed my sisters
 I ended up in a mall.

Bill Middleton

Often in a poem it is what is not said that is most important. We must ask the poem questions. Only then will a poem surrender its meaning.

Enfant

child
listen to father and mother
child
listen to brother and sister
child
cry not
break not
child
shout not
it's not nice
listen to what they say
listen to them they say
child
no one listens to you
it's best that way

Jacques Godbout

translated from the French
by John Robert Colombo

My Grandmother—The Bluebottle

The Chinese goddess rears her head again;
(I did not say it was ugly
though some might think so).

What made me think this
was my grandmother
A bluebottle
Buzzing around
Rubbing her legs together in glee
Watching us make constant
mockeries of ourselves;

She knows
and can see
that however we choose
to spend our mortal days
We too will end up like She—
rubbing, or buzzing
or humming in glee.

Bekleen Leong

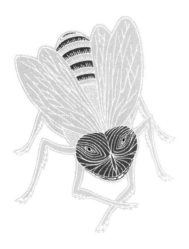

120 Miles North of Winnipeg

My grandfather came here years ago,
family of eight. In the village,
nine miles away, they knew him as
the German and they were suspicious, being
already settled. Later he was
somewhat liked; still later
forgotten. In winter everything
went white as buffalo bones and
the underwear froze on the line
10   like corpses. Often the youngest
was sick. Still he never thought
of leaving. Spring was always greener
than he'd known and summer had
kid-high grass with sunsets big
as God. The wheat was thick,
the log house chinked and warm.

The little English he spoke
he learned from the thin grey lady
in the one-room school, an hour away
20   by foot. The oldest could hunt, the youngest
could read. They knew nothing of
the world he'd left, and forgotten,
until 1914 made him an alien and
he left them on the land he'd come to,
120 miles north of Winnipeg.

Dale Zieroth

Poems are the heartbeat of the world.
Reading poems is like listening to your
own heart speaking.

War on the Periphery

Around the battlements go by
Soldier men against the sky,
Violent lovers, husbands, sons,
Guarding my peaceful life with guns.

My pleasures, how discreet they are!
A little booze, a little car,
Two little children and a wife
Living a small suburban life.

My little children eat my heart;
At seven o'clock we kiss and part,
At seven o'clock we meet again;
They eat my heart and grow to men.

I watch their tenderness with fear
While on the battlements I hear
The violent, obedient ones
Guarding my family with guns.

George Johnston

Proposition

Tonight
when the moon comes out
I shall change it
into money.

But I'd be sorry
if people knew about it,
for the moon
is an old family treasure.

Nicolás Guillén

**translated from the Spanish
by Langston Hughes**

"For whatever embryo the poem starts from—an event, an emotion, a character, a scene, an insight, an idea—its theme never exists in isolation."

Elizabeth Drew

Poems paint pictures with words. The language of poetry sketches the person, the scene, the object, the event.

A poet portrays the human condition and enlarges our capacity to see and to experience life in all its facets.

A poem
a plea, a pester,
a please,
a portrait,
a package of words.

Poems may be either private or public. The poem that is private sits you down and chats things over with you in the privacy of your heart. The poem that is public speaks with a louder voice, hoping to draw a crowd.

"The writer is both an eye-witness and I-witness, the one to whom personal experience happens and the one who makes experience personal for others."

Margaret Atwood

"Poetry is a kind of wild justice."

Susan Musgrave

The Unknown Citizen

(To JS/07/M/378
This Marble Monument
Is Erected by the State)

He was found by the Bureau of Statistics to be
One against whom there was no official complaint,
And all the reports on his conduct agree
That, in the modern sense of an old-fashioned word, he was a saint,
For in everything he did he served the Greater Community.
Except for the War till the day he retired
He worked in a factory and never got fired,
But satisfied his employers, Fudge Motors Inc.
Yet he wasn't a scab or odd in his views,
10   For his Union reports that he paid his dues,
(Our report on his Union shows it was sound)
And our Social Psychology workers found
That he was popular with his mates and liked a drink.
The Press are convinced that he bought a paper every day
And that his reactions to advertisements were normal in every way.
Policies taken out in his name prove that he was fully insured,
And his Health-card shows he was once in hospital but left it
       cured.
Both Producers Research and High-Grade Living declare
He was fully sensible to the advantages of the Instalment Plan
20   And had everything necessary to the Modern Man,
A phonograph, a radio, a car and a frigidaire.
Our researchers into Public Opinion are content
That he held the proper opinions for the time of year;
When there was peace, he was for peace; when there was war,
       he went.
He was married and added five children to the population,
Which our Eugenist says was the right number for a parent of
       his generation,

And our teachers report that he never interfered with their
   education.
Was he free? Was he happy? The question is absurd:
Had anything been wrong, we should certainly have heard.

W. H. Auden

Utopia — an ideal view of society, often
one only to be imagined.

Dystopia — an unfriendly, unpleasant,
grotesque, or ugly view of society.

The Average

His peasant parents killed themselves with toil
To let their darling leave a stingy soil
For any of those smart professions which
Encourage shallow breathing, and grow rich.

The pressure of their fond ambition made
Their shy and country-loving child afraid
No sensible career was good enough,
Only a hero could deserve such love.

So here he was without maps or supplies,
A hundred miles from any decent town;
The desert glared into his blood-shot eyes;

The silence roared displeasure: looking down,
He saw the shadow of an Average Man
Attempting the exceptional, and ran.

W. H. Auden

arren Pryor

When every pencil meant a sacrifice
his parents boarded him at school in town,
slaving to free him from the stony fields,
the meagre acreage that bore them down.

They blushed with pride when, at his graduation,
they watched him picking up the slender scroll,
his passport from the years of brutal toil
and lonely patience in a barren hole.

When he went in the Bank their cups ran over.
They marvelled how he wore a milk-white shirt
work days and jeans on Sundays. He was saved
from their thistle-strewn farm and its red dirt.

And he said nothing. Hard and serious
like a young bear inside his teller's cage,
his axe-hewn hands upon the paper bills
aching with empty strength and throttled rage.

Alden Nowlan

How He Turned Out

When he was young his parents saw (as parents by the million see)
That Rollo had an intellect of quite unequalled brilliancy;
They started in his training from the hour of his nativity,
And carefully they cultivated every bright proclivity.

At eight he ate up authors like a literary cannibal,
At nine he mastered Latin as the Latins mastered Hannibal,
At ten he knew astronomy and differential calculus,
And at eleven could dissect the tiniest animalculus.

At twelve he learned orthometry and started in to master all
The different kinds of poetry, the lyric and the pastoral,
The epic and dramatic, the descriptive and didactical,
With lessons theoretical and exercises practical.

Music he learned—the old and sweet, the up-to-date and hideous;
He painted like Apelles and he modelled like a Phidias;
In language he was polyglot, in rhetoric Johnsonian,
In eloquence Websterian, in diction Ciceronian.

At last, with learning that would set an ordinary head agog,
His education far outshone his most proficient pedagogue;
And so he entered life with all his lore to lift the lid for him—
And what do you imagine that his erudition did for him?

Alas! I fear the truth will shock you rather than amuse you all—
To those who read this kind of verse, the sequel is unusual.
This man (it's hard on humour, for it breaks the well-known laws of it)
Was happier for his learning, and a great success because of it.

Edwin Meade Robinson

Allusion — a casual reference to something or someone having historical, literary, or religious significance.

Night School

1. (Ernest Hearly)

i hear the teacher's
heels clinking
on the stone floor

i smile good night
pretending i'm brave

i sit in the back
so that she
won't see me
watching her

she catches my eye
and
i look at the wall

she comes down through
rows of desks
and takes my
hand

three gold rings
and herring scales.

Interior monologue — one
person's thoughts and
feelings: the stream of
consciousness.

2. (Noel Slaney)

i'm 56
and tired
of taking orders
from people
who don't give a damn
that i'm dying
shift by sweaty shift

when i'm done
what will they do
give me a pick and shovel
and tell me to dig
myself in

let me sit here
a while miss
where i won't hear
the rocks falling
in my grave.

3.   (Phonse Decker)

how can i learn
to write
when the pencil takes
crazy steps across
the page and my
hand shivers

i can swing the sledgehammer
and it
goes where i want
but the pencil
won't stay
with me

maybe i could do better if
my hands wouldn't
sweat.

4.   (Billy Hynes)

they say i'm crazy
because
i go to night school
but today i could read
all the names on all
the bloody cartons stacked
on the truck

i sat beside the driver
and smiled.

5.   (Miss Crowley)

how can I tell Ton Chung
that his skin is
the colour of
summer hay
his eyes like
brown spring pools
and when he speaks
I see butterflies
hovering over plum blossoms
    in a tea garden.

Len Margaret

Jazz

He's someone I know
who can play sax like no one I've ever heard.
His music seeps
and oozes
out of the cracks in his mind,
or it envelopes
          like a thousand screams
trying to unite.

Jazz is loud colour.

He plays like he's lived 9 lives plus one.
I listen to his song and learn.
Jazz knows all the rules
but, more importantly,
he knows how to break them.

Casey Elder

Lionel

Deadended at 53
Lionel lifts his cup
at a local back table.
He used to work, he says,
the trans-Atlantic run for P & O until
Parkinson's got him in the 60's but
if he had to do it again, he'd be a
jazz artist: percussion:
a slow salsa on the high hat;
laying down beat for the great sax;
smoky night clubs, lower east side…
"It would have been a cool gig,"
he sips, "but I guess you only get
what's been given."

Lionel's slight eyes watch
over tremoring hands as he
taps out his talent on a saucer.

David Duclos

Day of the Bride

The day of the bride dawns
Through layers of white plaster skin
And multi-sashed kimono
Head made huge by lacquered hair—
She is swept ashore in her glass bottle
White and tight as a folded paper message
Eyes hidden in a swirl of green boughs.
She moves like a mannequin
Manoeuvred by centuries of ceremony
Under the weight of speech and incantation
A wall of priests and watching families
Beside rows of low tables
With small triangles of paper
Congratulatory slits of squid and curls of seaweed.
Then kneeling at the bend of a fresh memory
She is discarded by her heavy day
And is plunged into the twentieth century
Tiny apartment daily stream
As a barely visible
Folded paper speck

Joy Kogawa

Neighbour

From across the street
we see her scissored
off by walls.
A hand quick as a lizard
takes in the milk
and once a week a sheet
weeps on the line.
That's all that's all
there is so why envy her?

Nutty old maid   spinster
crazy woman crazy woman
her silhouette balloons on silk
tassled blinds
private as a witch or a wizard
or a goddess, letting no one in,
choosing—that's the word—choosing no one.

Carol Shields

From the Inside Out

The person you see
is only part of me

she is brave
she is free
she lives
independently.

I can take her places
she fits in easily
her manners exemplary
parents like her
she likes to talk
she has degrees
and always some man
willing to accommodate
the love she gives
generously
but with discrimination.

The other one
I can't take anywhere
she bitches and swears
sees rain in sun
she cannot love
she is the one
behind the eyes.

Alice VanWart

Foil — contrast in character, setting, or action; to highlight one character's traits by showing a character with opposite traits.

hen I Think about Myself

When I think about myself,
I almost laugh myself to death,
My life has been one great big joke,
A dance that's walked
A song that's spoke,
I laugh so hard I almost choke
When I think about myself.

Sixty years in these folks' world
The child I works for calls me girl
I say "Yes ma'am" for working's sake.
Too proud to bend
Too poor to break,
I laugh until my stomach ache,
When I think about myself.

My folks can make me split my side,
I laughed so hard I nearly died,
The tales they tell, sound just like lying,
They grow the fruit,
But eat the rind,
I laugh until I start to crying,
When I think about my folks.

Maya Angelou

Chicago

Hog butcher for the World,
Tool Maker, Stacker of Wheat,
Player with Railroads and the Nation's
Freight Handler;
Stormy, husky, brawling,
City of Big Shoulders:

They tell me you are wicked and I believe them, for I have seen your
painted women under the gas lamps luring the farm boys.
And they tell me you are crooked and I answer: Yes, it is true I have
seen the gunmen kill and go free to kill again.
And they tell me you are brutal and my reply is: On the faces of
women and children I have seen the marks of wanton hunger.
And having answered so I turn once more to those who sneer at this
my city, and I give them back the sneer and say to them:
Come and show me another city with lifted head singing so proud to
be alive and coarse and strong and cunning.
Flinging magnetic curses amid the toil of piling job on job, here is
a tall bold slugger set vivid against the little soft cities;
Fierce as a dog with tongue lapping for action, cunning as a savage
pitted against the wilderness,
Bareheaded,
Shovelling,
Wrecking,
Planning,
Building, breaking, rebuilding,
Under the smoke, dust all over his mouth, laughing with white teeth,
Under the terrible burden of destiny laughing as a young man laughs,
Laughing even as an ignorant fighter laughs who has never lost a battle,
Bragging and laughing that under his wrist is the pulse, and under his
ribs the heart of the people,
Laughing!
Laughing the stormy, husky, brawling laughter of Youth, half-naked,
sweating, proud to be Hog Butcher, Tool Maker, Stacker of
Wheat, Player with Rail-roads and Freight Handler to the Nation.

Carl Sandburg

The Runaway

Once when the snow of the year was beginning to fall,
We stopped by a mountain pasture to say, "Whose colt?"
A little Morgan had one forefoot on the wall,
The other curled at his breast. He dipped his head
And snorted to us. And then he had to bolt.
We heard the miniature thunder where he fled,
And we saw him, or thought we saw him, dim and gray,
Like a shadow against the curtain of falling flakes.
"I think the little fellow's afraid of the snow.
10   He isn't winter-broken. It isn't play
With the little fellow at all. He's running away.
I doubt if even his mother could tell him, 'Sakes,
It's only weather.' He'd think she didn't know!
Where is his mother? He can't be out alone."
And now he comes again with a clatter of stone
And mounts the wall again with whited eyes
And all his tail that isn't hair up straight.
He shudders his coat as if to throw off flies.
"Whoever it is that leaves him out so late,
20   When other creatures have gone to stall and bin,
Ought to be told to come and take him in."

Robert Frost

Allegory — a story that has a
secondary meaning running along
with the surface story.

The Solitary Reaper

Behold her, single in the field,
   Yon solitary Highland lass!
Reaping and singing by herself;
   Stop here, or gently pass!
Alone she cuts and binds the grain,
And sings a melancholy strain;
O listen! for the vale profound
Is overflowing with the sound.

No nightingale did ever chaunt
   More welcome notes to weary bands
Of travellers in some shady haunt,
   Among Arabian sands:
A voice so thrilling ne'er was heard
In spring-time from the cuckoo-bird,
Breaking the silence of the seas
Among the farthest Hebrides.

Will no one tell me what she sings?—
   Perhaps the plaintive numbers flow
For old, unhappy, far-off things,
   And battles long ago:
Or is it some more humble lay,
Familiar matter of to-day?
Some natural sorrow, loss, or pain,
That has been, and may be again?

Whate'er the theme, the maiden sang
   As if her song could have no ending;
I saw her singing at her work,
   And o'er the sickle bending;—
I listened, motionless and still;
And, as I mounted up the hill,
The music in my heart I bore,
Long after it was heard no more.

William Wordsworth

Edith

My aunt died last week,
She was old, and had been sick for a long time.
It's better this way, they said, but the daughters cried,
And the sons said nothing.

I could not, of course, remember her young.
She was forty-five when I was born.
Auntie she had always been to me,
But her name was Edith.

I looked at her secret face and smelled the flowers,
She always liked flowers,
Then I sat in the church
And the organ lulled me.

But something made me remember
An old man I met on the bus one day
Who asked me about my people
As old men will.

He listened, nodding approval
Glad he could place me in his shrinking world,
And then, as he was leaving
He turned and said:

The next time you see Ede Ebsary
Tell her Tom Hayes was askin' about her.
She was a lovely-lookin' girl,
All there for a bit of fun.

The preacher announced the hymn and I thought of Edith,
Not Auntie or Mother or Nan
I never did tell her because she was very deaf
And she probably wouldn't have heard me.

Helen Porter

The Tramp

Open wide the door—
What does it matter
That his dusty clothes
Are all a-tatter?
He carries moonlight
On his shoulder—
Open wide the door,
The night grows colder.
Heap the hearth fire,
Seat the stranger near.
Do not cringe, children,
There's naught to fear—
Though he comes and goes
With an alien tongue,
On his ragged sleeve
A thrush has sung.

Martha Ostenso

Dream Variations

To fling my arms wide
In some place of the sun,
To whirl and to dance
Till the white day is done.
Then rest at cool evening
Beneath a tall tree
While night comes on gently,
     Dark like me—
That is my dream!

To fling my arms wide
In the face of the sun,
Dance! Whirl! Whirl!
Till the quick day is done.
Rest at pale evening…
A tall, slim tree…
Night coming tenderly
     Black like me.

Langston Hughes

"Poetry is the music of words, reaching further than words alone could."

Colin Dueck

The poem as song.

Every day thousands of poems are transformed into pure energy to ride out on the airwaves. Have you tuned in to a good poem lately?

The lyrics of the song should be able to stand alone without the music. What are the songs saying? Is there a message as well as a beat?

"The poet's craft is to turn words into deeds."

Elizabeth Drew

uthering Heights

Out on the wily, windy moors
We'd roll and fall in green
You had a temper, like my jealousy
Too hot, too greedy
How could you leave me?
When I needed to possess you
I hated you, I loved you too

Bad dreams in the night
They told me I was going to lose the fight
Leave behind my wuthering, wuthering
Wuthering Heights

Heathcliff, it's me, Cathy, come home
I'm so cold, let me in-a-your window

Oh it gets dark, it gets lonely
On the other side from you
I pine a lot, I find the lot
Falls through without you
I'm coming back love, cruel Heathcliff
My one dream, my only master

Too long I roam in the night
I'm coming back to his side to put it right
I'm coming home to wuthering, wuthering
Wuthering Heights

Heathcliff, it's me, Cathy, come home
I'm so cold, let me in-a-your window

Oh let me have it, let me grab your soul away
You know it's me, Cathy

Heathcliff, it's me, Cathy, come home
I'm so cold, let me in-a-your window

Kate Bush

A Spaceman Came Travelling...

A spaceman came travelling on his ship from afar,
'Twas light years of time since his mission did start,
And over a village he halted his craft,
And it hung in the sky like a star, just like a star...

He followed a light and came down to a shed,
Where a mother and child were lying there on a bed,
A bright light of silver shone round his head,
And he had the face of an angel, and they were afraid...

Then the stranger spoke, he said "Do not fear,
I come from a planet a long way from here,
And I bring a message for mankind to hear,"
And suddenly the sweetest music filled the air...

    And it went La La...
    Peace and goodwill to all men, and love for the child...

This lovely music went trembling through the ground,
And many were wakened on hearing that sound,
And travellers on the road, the village they found,
By the light of that ship in the sky which shone all around...

And just before dawn at the paling of the sky,
The stranger returned and said "Now I must fly,
When two thousand years of your time has gone by,
This song will begin once again, to a baby's cry..."

    And it went La La...This song will begin once again
    to a baby's cry...
    And it goes La La...Peace and goodwill to all men, and
    love for the child...
    Oh the whole world is waiting, waiting to
    hear the song again,
    There are thousands standing on the edge of the world,
    And a star is moving somewhere, the time is nearly here,
    This song will begin once again, to a baby's cry...

Chris De Burgh

(Nothing But)
Flowers

Here we stand
Like an Adam and an Eve
Waterfalls
The Garden of Eden
Two fools in love
So beautiful and strong
The birds in the trees
Are smiling upon them
From the age of the dinosaurs
Cars have run on gasoline
Where, where have they gone?
Now, it's nothing but flowers

There was a factory
Now there are mountains and rivers
We caught a rattlesnake
Now we got something for dinner
There was a shopping mall
Now it's all covered with flowers
If this is paradise
I wish I had a lawnmower

Years ago
I was an angry young man
I'd pretend
That I was a billboard
Standing tall
By the side of the road
I fell in love
With a beautiful highway

This used to be real estate
Now it's only fields and trees
Where, where is the town?
Now, it's nothing but flowers
The highways and the cars
Were sacrificed for agriculture
I thought that we'd start over
But I guess I was wrong

Once there were parking lots
    Now it's a peaceful oasis
This was a Pizza Hut
    Now it's all covered with daisies
I miss the honky tonks,
    Dairy Queens and 7-Elevens
And as things fell apart
    Nobody paid much attention
I dream of cherry pies,
    Candy bars and chocolate chip cookies
We used to microwave,
    Now we just eat nuts and berries
This was a discount store,
    Now it's turned into a cornfield
Don't leave me stranded here,
    I can't get used to this lifestyle

performed by Talking Heads

David Byrne

The Sound of Silence

Hello darkness my old friend,
I've come to talk with you again,
Because a vision softly creeping,
Left its seeds while I was sleeping
And the vision that was planted in my brain
Still remains within the sound of silence.

In restless dreams I walked alone,
Narrow streets of cobble stone
'Neath the halo of a street lamp,
I turned my collar to the cold and damp
When my eyes were stabbed by the flash of a neon light
That split the night, and touched the sound of silence.

And in the naked light I saw
Ten thousand people maybe more,
People talking without speaking,
People hearing without listening,
People writing songs that voices never share
And no one dares disturb the sound of silence.

"Fools!" said I, "You do not know
Silence like a cancer grows
Hear my words that I might teach you
Take my arms that I might reach you."
But my words like silent raindrops fell
And echoed, in the wells of silence.

And the people bowed and prayed
To the neon God they made,
And the sign flashed out its warning
In the words that it was forming.
And the sign said:
      "The words of the prophets are written
         on the subway walls and tenement halls"
And whispered in the sounds of silence.

performed by Simon and Garfunkel

Paul Simon

Four Strong Winds

Four strong winds that blow lonely,
Seven seas that run high,
All those things that don't change come what may—
But our good times are all gone
And I'm bound for movin' on,
I'll look for you if I'm ever back this way—

I think I'll go out to Alberta—
Weather's good there in the fall,
I got some friends that I can go to workin' for—
Still I wish you'd change your mind
If I asked you one more time
But we've been through that a hundred times or more—

Four strong winds that blow lonely,
Seven seas that run high,
All those things that don't change come what may—
But our good times are all gone
And I'm bound for movin' on,
I'll look for you if I'm ever back this way—

If I get there before the snow flies
And if things are goin' good,
You could meet me if I sent you down the fare.
But, by then it would be winter,
Ain't too much for you to do
And those winds sure can blow cold way out there.

Four strong winds that blow lonely,
Seven seas that run high,
All those things that don't change come what may—
But our good times are all gone
And I'm bound for movin' on,
I'll look for you if I'm ever back this way—

performed by Ian and Sylvia

Ian Tyson

orking Man

It's a working man I am
And I've been down under ground
And I swear to God if I ever see the sun
Or for any length of time
I can hold it in my mind
I never again will go down under ground

At the age of sixteen years
Oh he quarrels with his peers
Who vowed they'd never see another one
In the dark recess of the mines
Where you age before your time
And the coal dust lies heavy on your lungs

At the age of sixty-four
Oh he'll greet you at the door
And he'll gently lead you by the arm
Through the dark recess of the mines
Oh he'll take you back in time
And he'll tell you of the hardships that were had

It's a working man I am
And I've been down under ground
And I swear to God if I ever see the sun
Or for any length of time
I can hold it in my mind
I never again will go down under ground

God I never again will go down under ground

Rita MacNeil

Realized Your Dreams

So you never left the small town
With your friends when things got way down
You stood between the tall trees
Threw all caution to the cool breeze
You stayed home on the island
And you watched the evening sunrise
And you never thought of leaving
Even when the winds blew cold

And I've seen you at the station
With your arms outstretched and waiting
To welcome home the travellers
Who went searching after dreams
And they never fail to mention
How your life's been one dimension
And you smile at good intentions
Knowing well they'll never see

All you want or ever needed
You found here without leaving
It's the drifter and the dreamer
Who often fail to see
In the heart that never wanders
Lies a peace that comes with morning
It's knowing when the day is done
You've realized your dreams

So you never left the old ties
When the changing winds came by
You walked beside the old mill
Turned your eyes upon the green hill
And you stayed home on the island
And you watched the loved ones follow
All the roads that led them searching
After ordinary dreams

Rita MacNeil

191

r. Tanner

Mr. Tanner was a cleaner from a town in the Midwest. Of all the cleaning shops around he'd made his the best. He also was a baritone who sang while hanging clothes. He practised scales while pressing tails and sang at local shows. His friends and neighbours praised the voice that poured out from his throat. They said that he should use his gift instead of cleaning coats. But music was his life, it was not his livelihood, and it made him feel so happy, and it made him feel so good. He sang from his heart and he sang from his soul. He did not know how well he sang, it just made him whole. His friends kept working on him to try music out full time, a big debut and rave reviews, a great career to climb. Finally they got to him, he would take the fling. A concert agent in New York agreed to have him sing. There were plane tickets, phone calls, money spent to rent the hall. It took most of his savings, but he'd gladly used them all. The evening came, he took the stage, his face set in a smile. In the half-filled hall the critics sat watching on the aisle. The concert was a blur to him, spatters of applause. He did not know how well he'd sang, he only heard the flaws. But the critics were concise, it only took four lines, and no one could accuse them of being overkind. "Mr. Martin Tanner, baritone, of Dayton, Ohio, made his town hall debut last night. He came well prepared, but unfortunately his presentation was not up to contemporary professional standards. His voice lacks the range of tonal colour necessary to make it consistently interesting. Full time consideration of another endeavour might be in order." He came home to Dayton and was questioned by his friends. But he smiled and just said nothing and he never sang again, excepting very late at night when the shop was dark and closed, he sang softly to himself as he sorted through the clothes.

Harry Chapin

Circle

All my life's a circle, sunrise and sundown.
The moon rolls through the nighttime, 'til
the daybreak comes around. All my life's a
circle, but I can't tell you why. The seasons
spinning 'round again, the years keep on
rolling by. Seems like I've been here before,
I can't remember when. But I've got this
funny feeling, that I'll be back once again.
No straight lines make up my life and all my
roads have bends. There's no clear cut
beginnings, and so far no dead ends. I've
found you a thousand times, I guess you've
done the same. But then we lose each other,
it's just like a children's game. And as I see
you here again, the thought runs through
my mind: our love is like a circle, let's go
'round one more time.

Harry Chapin

"A great poem is for ages and ages
in common and for all degrees and
complexions and all departments
and sects and for a woman as
much as a man and a man as much
as a woman. A great poem is no
finish to a man or woman but rather
a beginning."

Walt Whitman

Vincent

Starry, starry night, paint your palette blue and grey,
Look out on a summer's day, with eyes that know the darkness in my soul.
Shadows on the hills, sketch the trees and daffodils,
Catch the breeze and the winter chills,
In colours on the snowy linen land.

> And now I understand what you tried to say to me,
> How you suffered for your sanity,
> How you tried to set them free.
> They would not listen, they did not know how,—
> Perhaps they'll listen now.

Starry, starry night, flaming flow'rs that brightly blaze,
Swirling clouds in violet haze reflect in Vincent's eyes of China blue.
Colours changing hue, morning fields of amber grain,
Weathered faces lined in pain,
Are soothed beneath the artist's loving hand.

> And now I understand what you tried to say to me,
> How you suffered for your sanity,
> How you tried to set them free.
> They would not listen, they did not know how,—
> Perhaps they'll listen now.

For they could not love you,
But still your love was true,
And when no hope was left in sight on that starry, starry night,
You took your life, as lovers often do;
But I could have told you, Vincent,
This world was never meant for one as beautiful as you.

Starry, starry night, portraits hung in empty halls,
Frameless heads on nameless walls, with eyes that watch the world
       and can't forget.
Like the strangers that you've met, the ragged men in ragged clothes,
The silver thorn of bloody rose,
Lie crushed and broken on the virgin snow.

And now I think I know what you tried to say to me,
How you suffered for your sanity,
How you tried to set them free.
They would not listen,
They're not list'ning still,—
Perhaps they never will.

Don McLean

from Red and Black

ENJOLRAS
It is time for us all
To decide who we are
Do we fight for the right
To a night at the opera now?
Have you asked of yourselves
What's the price you might pay?
Is it simply a game
For rich young boys to play?
The colour of the world
Is changing day by day…
Red—the blood of angry men!
Black—the dark of ages past!
Red—a world about to dawn!
Black—the night that ends at last!

MARIUS
Had you been there tonight
You might know how it feels
To be struck to the bone
In a moment of breathless delight!
Had you been there tonight
You might also have known
How the world may be changed
In just one burst of light
And what was right seems wrong
And what was wrong seems right!
Red—I feel my soul on fire!
Black—my world if she's not there!
Red—the colour of desire!
Black—the colour of despair!

ENJOLRAS
Marius, you're no longer a child
I do not doubt you mean it well
But now there is a higher call.
Who cares about your lonely soul?
We strive towards a larger goal
Our little lives don't count at all!

STUDENTS
Red—the blood of angry men!
Black—the dark of ages past!
Red—a world about to dawn!
Black—the night that ends at last!

Music by Claude-Michel Schönberg

Words by Herber Kretzmer

I Dreamed a Dream

There was a time when men were kind,
When their voices were soft
And their words inviting.
There was a time when love was blind
And the world was a song
And the song was exciting.
There was a time.
Then it all went wrong.
I dreamed a dream in time gone by
When hope was high
And life worth living
I dreamed that love would never die
I dreamed that God would be forgiving.
Then I was young and unafraid
And dreams were made and used
And wasted
There was no ransom to be paid
No song unsung
No wine untasted.
But the tigers come at night
With their voices soft as thunder
As they tear your hope apart
As they turn your dream to shame.
He slept a summer by my side

He filled my days
With endless wonder
He took my childhood in his stride
But he was gone when autumn came.
And still I dream he'll come to me
That we will live the years together
But there are dreams that cannot be
And there are storms
We cannot weather…
I had a dream my life would be
So different form this hell I'm living
So different now from what it seemed
Now life has killed
The dream I dreamed.

Music by Claude-Michel Schönberg

Words by Herbert Kretzmer

Sit Down Young Stranger

I'm standing at the doorway, my head down in my hands,
Not knowing where to sit, not knowing where I stand,
My father looms above me, for him there is no rest,
My mother's arms enfold me and hold me to her breast,
"They say you've been out wanderin', they say you've travelled far,
Sit down young stranger and tell us who you are."

The room has all gone misty, my thoughts are all in spin,
"Sit down young stranger and tell us where you been,"
"Well I been out to the mountain, I walked down by the sea,
I never questioned no one questioned me,
My love was given freely and oft-times it was returned,
I never came to borrow, I only came to learn.
Sometimes it did get lonely but it taught me how to cry,
And laughter came to me easy for life to pass me by,
I never had a dollar that I didn't earn with pride,
'Cause I had a million daydreams to keep me satisfied."

"And will you gather daydreams or will you gather wealth?"
"How can you find your fortune when you cannot find yourself?"
My mother's eyes are misty, there's a trembling in her hand,
"Sit down young stranger I do not understand,
And will you try and tell us you been too long at school,
And knowledge is not needed, that power does not rule,
That war is not the answer, that young men should not die,
Sit down young stranger, I wait for your reply."

"The answer is not easy for souls are not reborn,
To wear a crown of peace you must wear a crown of thorns
If Jesus had a reason I'm sure he would not tell,
They treated him so badly how could he wish them well?"

The parlour now is empty, there's nothing left to say,
My father has departed, my mother's gone to pray.
There's rockets in the meadows and ships out on the sea,
The answer's in the forest, carved upon a tree.

John loves Mary, does anyone love me?

Gordon Lightfoot

My Hometown

I was eight years old and running with a dime in my hand
into the bus stop to pick up a paper for my old man
I'd sit on his lap in that big old Buick and steer as we
drove through town
He'd tousle my hair and say son take a good look around
this is your hometown
This is your hometown

In '65 tension was running high, at my high school
There was a lot of fights between the black and white
There was nothing you could do
Two cars at a light on a Saturday night, in the back
seat there was a gun
Words were passed, in a shotgun blast
Troubled times had come, to my hometown
My hometown

Now Main Street's whitewashed windows and vacant stores
seems like there ain't nobody wants to come down
here no more
They're closing down the textile mill across
the railroad tracks
Foreman says these jobs are going boys and they ain't
coming back to your hometown
Your hometown

Last night me and Kate we laid in bed talking about
getting out
Packing up our bags maybe heading south
I'm 35, we got a boy of our own now
Last night I sat him up, behind the wheel and said
son take a good look around, this is your hometown
This is your hometown

Bruce Springsteen

Unnatural Causes

The wind howled and cussed
it knew no rest
when it ran free
it was a hurricane
to be watched and silenced

silence makes you sit and rot
even cactus fades
against persistent drought

they hope the poor will become acclimatized
see how they look at skyrises
and call them mountain peaks
see how the sun greets them first
in the city
makes a rolling shadow

Somewhere in this silvered city
hunger rails beneath the flesh
…and one by one, they're closing shops in the city
…the Epicure, the Rivoli on the porch…
No Small Affair
…No Small Affair—the Sequel…La Petit Café
The Bamboo…

The city, a curtained metropolitan glare
grins a diamond sparkle sunset
it cuts a dashing pose

"The picture you sent on the postcard was wonderful!
It reminded me of a fairy land,
where everything is so clean
a place where everyone is happy
and well taken care of
…and the sky…the sky…it seems so round, so huge
and so indifferent."

Indifference passes through the wind
the wind, it rains a new breed
breeds a new passion
the passion of inaction
the inaction of politicians
the art of avoiding issues
the issues of culture
the culture of exclusion
the exclusion of the "political" and the powerless

Somewhere in this our city
in our governing chambers
a watershed of indelight
of neutered niceties, unctuous
Click////click////click
postcard perfect

Dry rivers in the valley
the thirst at the banks of plenty
the room at the street-car shelter
a bus stop bed
a bus stop bed
a bus stop bed

You can make it through winter if you're ice
You can make it through winter if you're ice

gone frozen
on many things
bare back. no shelter
iced hearts in the elements
impassioned is the wind

All people are created equal except in winter
All people are created equal except in winter

Right here
on the front steps of abundance

Caroline Bungle tugs her load
stakes a place, invites a little company of sleep
unclick////
this my dear is very unpostcardlike

Not inclined to poses
posturing only her plight
a dungle of terror
of lost hope
abandonment
an explorer in the arctic of our culture
a straggler adrift
cross our terrain of indifference
a life unravelled
seeks a connection
a soul outstretched to the cosmos

Can you spare a little social change, please?
a cup of tea
  a cup of tea
a place to sleep
a job
  a job
    a job…????

"The last postcard you sent was kinda weird
…poor people, sleeping at the bus stop!??
Surely you don't have that there…"

"…anyways, I'm dying to come to Canada
I'm a pioneer!"

Lillian Allen

> "The writer wants his pen to turn stone into sunlight, language into fire."
>
> **Bernard Malamud**

This section contains poems about reading and writing poetry.

Poetry appeals to that artistic side of us that wants to make things of beauty out of the raw material of life's experiences.

Poets are workers with words. They must free the words to soar on the wings of the dawn. They must "turn stone into sunlight" and "language into fire."

The Artist and the Creative Process

The musician—makes a statement in melody and harmony
The painter—uses line and colour
The sculptor—creates with form and dimension
The poet—is the artisan using words
The dancer—speaks through movement

Write your own definition of poetry...

> "Poetry is a crushed rose floating in the muddy puddle outside my window."
>
> **Tara Zahar**

> "The best words in their best order."
>
> **Samuel Taylor Coleridge**

[You are reading this too fast.]

You are reading this too fast.
Slow down, for this is poetry
and poetry works slowly.
Unless you live with it a while
the spirit will never descend.
It's so easy to quickly cut across the surface
and then claim there was nothing to find.
Touch the poem gently with your eyes
just you would touch a lover's flesh.
10   Poetry is an exercise in patience,
you must wait for it to come to you.
The spirit manifests in many guises;
some quiver with beauty,
some vibrate with song.
What is happening?
Slow down, slow down,
take a few deep breaths,
read the poem slowly,
read the lines one at a time,
20   read the words one by one,
read the spaces between the words,
get sleepy, this is poetry,
relax until your heart
is vulnerable, wide open.

Ken Norris

"One reads poetry with one's nerves."
Wallace Stevens

The Word Game

by this time i am speaking to the reader
who has found his or her way somehow almost
to the end of this book.

anyone else can read this too,
but i am not really talking with them,
i am talking with people

who got here by a beautiful kind of patience
who got here by beautifully understanding
or who got here by a beautiful kind of anger,

listen, i have a suggestion for a game for you.
write a poem in twenty minutes,
like this one was.

don't leave poetry to the poets,
don't try to write a poem,
write one.

just pick up a pencil & write one.

Richard Sommer

"All there is to writing is having ideas. To learn to write is to learn to have ideas."
Robert Frost

"It is tremendously important that great poetry be written, it makes no jot of difference who writes it."
Ezra Pound

Greatness

I would be the greatest poet the world has ever known
if only I could make you see
here on the page
sunlight
a sparrow
three kernels of popcorn
spilled on the snow.

Alden Nowlan

An Exchange of Gifts

As long as you read this poem
I will be writing it.
I am writing it here and now
before your eyes,
although you can't see me.
Perhaps you'll dismiss this
as a verbal trick,
the joke is you're wrong;
the real trick
is your pretending
this is something
fixed and solid,
external to us both.
I tell you better:
I will keep on
writing this poem for you
even after I'm dead.

Alden Nowlan

"A good poet is someone who manages, in a lifetime of standing out in thunderstorms, to be struck by lightning five or six times; a dozen or two dozen times and he is great."

Robin Skelton

Saint Francis and the Birds

When Francis preached love to the birds
They listened, fluttered, throttled up
Into the blue like a flock of words

Released for fun from his holy lips.
Then wheeled back, whirred about his head,
Pirouetted on brothers' capes,

Danced on the wing, for sheer joy played
And sang, like images took flight.
Which was the best poem Francis made,

His argument true, his tone light.

Seamus Heaney

Mice in the House

One of them scampers down the curtain
and up to my motionless feet—
I have the feeling watching that
representatives of two powerful races
are meeting here calmly as equals—
But the mouse will not be damn fool enough
                to go away and write a poem—

Al Purdy

The Grand Dance

I promised I would never turn you into poetry, but
Allow this liar these wilful, wicked lines.

I am simply trying to track you down
In preworlds and afterworlds
And the present myriad inner worlds
Which whirl around in the carousel of space.

I hurl breathless poems against my lord Death,
Send these words, these words
Careening into the beautiful darkness.

10   And where do all the words go?
They say that somewhere out there in space
Every word uttered by every man
Since the beginning of man
Is still sounding. Afterthoughts,

Lethal gossip of the spheres.

Dance then, dance in the city streets,
Your body a fierce illusion of flesh, of energy,
The particles of light cast off from your hair
Illumine you for this moment only.

20   Your afterimage claims the air
And every moment is Apocalypse—

Avatar, deathless
Anarchy.

Gwendolyn MacEwen

Diction — the choice of words. The poet selects
each word carefully to express her meaning.

Ars Poetica

A poem should be palpable and mute
As a globed fruit

Dumb
As old medallions to the thumb

Silent as the sleeve-worn stone
Of casement ledges where the moss has grown—

A poem should be wordless
As the flight of birds

A poem should be motionless in time
As the moon climbs

Leaving, as the moon releases
Twig by twig the night-entangled trees,

Leaving, as the moon behind the winter leaves,
Memory by memory the mind—

A poem should be motionless in time
As the moon climbs

A poem should be equal to:
Not true

For all the history of grief
An empty doorway and a maple leaf

For love
The leaning grasses and two lights above the sea—

A poem should not mean
But be.

Archibald MacLeish

The Secret

Two girls discover
the secret of life
in a sudden line of
poetry.

I who don't know the
secret wrote
the line. They
told me

(through a third person)
they had found it
but not what it was
not even

what line it was. No doubt
by now, more than a week
later, they have forgotten
the secret,

the line, the name of
the poem. I love them
for finding what
I can't find,

and for loving me
for the line I wrote,
and for forgetting it
so that

a thousand times, till death
finds them, they may
discover it again, in other
lines

in other
happenings. And for
wanting to know it,
for

assuming there is
such a secret, yes,
for that
most of all.

Denise Levertov

"The ideal reader must be sensitive to words over their whole poetic range, and respond to poetry musically, emotionally, imaginatively."

Katherine M. Wilson

Alphabet Poem

A poem using the linear order of the letters of the alphabet at the start of each line. Usually the poet works with only a portion of the alphabet:

> Age
> Birth
> Coffin
> Desire
> Eternity

Alliteration

The repetition of initial sounds in words.
"For soft is the song my paddle sings."
> E. Pauline Johnson

Allusion

A reference to something or some person from literature, religious lore, or history. In "Rumours of War" by Pat Lowther there are several allusions to World War II (1939-1945).

Anapest

(∪ ∪ ∕) (interrupt) A poetic foot. An anapest consists of two short syllables followed by a stressed syllable.

Antithesis

Contrasting ideas expressed in a balanced grammatical structure.
"it is better to be happy
for a moment
and be burned up by beauty
than to live a long time

and be bored all the while"
> Don Marquis

Apostrophe

To address a person or thing not present as if it were present.
"Hello darkness my old friend"
> Paul Simon

Archetype

("the original type") A basic pattern or concept common to people of different times and cultures. For example, most peoples have a traditional story about how the world was created.

Art Trouvé

Found art. Found poetry. Ready-made art. Anti-art. Poems made from newspaper headlines and other non-poetic print are a form of art trouvé.

Artistic Click

What the reader experiences when the elements of the poem snap into place and make perfect sense. The feeling of understanding that leads to inspiration.

Assonance

Repetition of the same vowel sound in a line of poetry.
"Why he left his home in the South to roam round the Pole, God only knows."
> Robert Service

Atmosphere
See **Mood**.

Audience
Those who watch, read, listen, enjoy, judge. The people for whom the work was intended.

Audio
(Latin = I hear) Audio refers to the sound portion of a film, a TV broadcast—or a poem. How does a poem speak?

Avant-garde
(French = advance guard) The term refers to those artists who are innovators in thought, style, and form. See the chapter "Poetry 3000."

Ballad
A narrative poem, originally composed to be sung. "The Ballad of Birmingham" is a ballad.

Black Humour
In literature, a style of writing that finds humour in serious topics such as cruelty, insanity, murder, death, and other painful realities. See "equal opportunity" by Jim Wong-Chu.

Cacophony
The use of sounds that are unpleasant to the ear.
"Dirty British coaster with a salt-caked smoke-stack,"

John Masefield

Calligram
The lines of the poem are arranged in the shape of the subject of the poem. Also called shape poetry or pattern poetry. See "Calligram, 15 May 1915" by Guillaume Apollinaire.

Chorus
A line or stanza that is regularly repeated throughout a song. A chorus is the musical equivalent of a refrain.

Cinepoem
A poem that imitates the frames of a movie (the cinema). See Decio Pignatari's "LIFE."

Collage
A work of art made of objects and substances from many different sources. The artist collects, selects, and arranges the materials.

Computer poetry
The poet takes a word or phrase and works toward a readout. Each line of the poem consists of letters selected from the initial word or phrase; each letter remains in its original position. See "Sweethearts" by Emmett Williams.

Concrete Poetry
Poetry that places attention on the concrete material out of which the poem is made—letters and words. The appeal is to the visual, phonetic, and kinetic. See pages 135-152.

Connotation

The aura, the field of association, surrounding the word. Margaret Atwood's "Night Poem" evokes the atmosphere of the swamp, with its mildew, decay, stagnation, and mystery—"its beige moon damp as a mushroom/its drowned stumps and long birds."

Consonance

The repetition of identical consonant sounds.
"Shadows on the hills, sketch the trees and the daffodils"

Don McLean

Convention

A time-honoured way of doing something. By convention, a limerick has five lines.

Couplet

Two successive lines of poetry that rhyme.

cummingese

A word coined to describe the poetic language developed by Edward Estlin Cummings (1894-1962). Cummings wrote poems for the eye as well as the ear. See pages 124-125.

Dactyl

($/\ \cup\ \cup$) (merrily) A poetic foot. A dactyl contains three syllables, with the accent on the first syllable.

Denotation

The exact dictionary definition of a word.

Dialect

The language of a special group or class of people. "Edward, Edward," a ballad, is written in an old Scottish dialect.

Dialogue

A conversation, a talking to each other. See Christina Rossetti's poem "Uphill," written as a question-and-answer dialogue between two unnamed speakers.

Diction

The words the poet chooses to express his or her meaning. A good poet selects each word carefully, for a particular reason.

Didactic Verse

Poetry written to instruct or teach. See Lillian Allen's "Unnatural Causes."

Disc Poetry

Songs that have poetic merit that one hears on the radio airwaves or on CDs, cassettes, and records.

Elegy

A lyric poem of a mournful nature written about someone's death. "Break, Break, Break" by Alfred, Lord Tennyson is elegiac.

Emotive Language

Language that evokes an emotional response in the reader. The language of poetry is emotive. Poetry makes reference to facts and depicts objects and situations, but it also strongly appeals to attitudes and feelings.

Epigram

A very short poem, often consisting of two rhyming lines. Epigrams are usually satirical, wise, or witty. See "Against Broccoli" by Roy Blount, Jr.

Epiphany

A moment of sudden insight or revelation. See Fred Wah's "my father hurt—."

Euphemism

The use of a pleasant-sounding word or phrase to avoid talking about the unpleasant reality. "Die" is the precise real word. Euphemisms for die are "passed away," "gone to his reward," "no longer with us."

Euphony

The use of sounds pleasing to the ear. The combination of pleasant sounds in speech, poetry, or music.
"They listened, fluttered, throttled up Into the blue like a flock of words"

Seamus Heaney

Eye Rhyme

Words that rhyme to the eye but not to the ear: stood/blood; gave/have.

Feminine Rhyme

Rhymes of two syllables are called feminine rhymes: deliver/quiver; grieving/believing.

Figurative Language

Heightened, imaginative language, characterized by simile, metaphor, personification, and so on.
"Someone's shoes chewing an icy path."

Roo Borson

Flashback

A pause in the narrative flow to relate events from the past. These retreats to the past have a bearing on the present situation. See "The Battle of Blenheim" by Robert Southey.

Foil

Contrast in character, setting, or action. The writer emphasizes or enhances one character's traits by playing him or her off against a character with opposite qualities. See "From the Inside Out" by Alice VanWart.

Foot

The smallest combination of accented and unaccented syllables in a line of poetry. A line of verse usually has several feet.

Foreshadowing

Indicating or suggesting before it happens what will occur later in the work of art.

Form

The pattern or the structure of the poem; the way the poem is put together. Some poems take the form of a story, a narrative. Others are structured like a dialogue or an argument. Others like a work of music. Others are put together in a more intuitive way, in a succession of related images, for example. Form ≠ genre.

Free Verse

(also known as vers libre) Free verse follows the natural cadences of the language and discards traditional metre, rhyme, and stanza patterns. See Raymond Souster's "The Launching."

Genre

A certain kind of literature or poetry. The novel is a literary genre. Poetic genres include the sonnet, the lyric, and the haiku. Each genre is characterized by a set of rules or conventions that provides the parameters of the poem. Genre is a convenient but sometimes misleading and unhelpful way of classifying poetry. Is "The Wind Disturbs" by D. G. Jones a haiku?

Global Village

Marshall McLuhan (1911-1980) coined this term to suggest that the information explosion of the high-tech era was turning the world into one main street, one global village. The spread of film, radio, and TV had annihilated distance. See Duke Redbird's concrete poem "Indian Concepts."

Gothic

The atmosphere of the horror story, replete with ghosts, mystery, horrible happenings, and the macabre. "Flannan Isle" by Wilfrid Wilson Gibson has the gothic mood.

Haiku

Originally a genre of Japanese poetry. The haiku is usually written in 3 lines, containing 17 syllables. The organization of syllables (5-7-5) represents one flowing out of the spirit into one exhalation of breath. See pages 130-131.

Hyperbole

Obvious exaggeration of the facts either for a comic or serious effect. See Don Domanski's "Flea."

Iamb

(⌣ ⁄) (destróy) A poetic foot. An iamb has two syllables, with the stress on the second syllable. Iambic rhythm is the most common metre in English poetry.

Image

A word picture. An appeal to the reader's senses and imagination.

Imagery

All the images in the poem considered as a whole. A poem's imagery creates a certain mood. It suggests to the reader what to think and feel, often very subtly.

"in medias res"

Many works of art tell a story, but sometimes the artist doesn't want to begin at the beginning or end at the end. "In medias res" is a Latin expression meaning "in the middle of things," which is where some narratives start.

Interior Monologue

One person's inner thoughts and feelings. The flow of thoughts or the stream of consciousness is sometimes linear and sometimes a non-linear weaving of inner realities. See Helen Porter's "The Dancer."

Irony

Irony occurs when someone says something but the reverse is true, or when a situation appears to be one way but instead is exactly the opposite. "next to of course god" by e. e. cummings is an ironic portrait of a "patriotic" politician.

Juxtaposition

The poet puts two or more things side-by-side, even though they usually aren't associated with one another. The poet creates the juxtaposition without explaining it. The reader has to employ his or her imagination to guess at the poet's motives.

"Like a small grey
coffeepot
sits the squirrel."
                              Humbert Wolfe

Lampoon

A poem that satirizes a person by sketching a malicious character portrait. See "What the Defence-Plant Worker Said" by Bonnie Day.

Light Verse

Poetry whose main purpose is to delight and entertain. See the chapter "Poems on the Lighter Side."

Limerick

A five-line poem rhyming aabba and written in anapestic metre. This verse form has been popular since the 1846 publication of Edward Lear's *Book of Nonsense Verse*. See "There was a young lady of Spain."

Literal

An interpretation of a poem not going beyond the actual facts. An interpretation based wholly on the actual meaning of the words and lines. A literal interpretation ignores the potential of figurative language, imagery, symbolism, and leaps of imagination.

Lyric
A broad poetic category or genre. A lyric is a short poem expressing a personal feeling, emotion, or attitude about some topic.

Masculine Rhyme
Single-syllable rhymes are masculine rhymes:
light/night; song/wrong.

The Medium is the Message
A phrase coined by Canadian philosopher Marshall McLuhan. *How* something is said is more important than *what* is said. See the chapter entitled "Poetry 3000."

Metaphor
A comparison between two unlike things. The poet actually identifies one thing with another, asserting that they are the same.
"Jazz is loud colour."

Casey Elder

Metre
Metre (measure) depends on the number of feet in a given line of poetry. Rhythm is determined by the pattern of stressed and unstressed syllables in a line of poetry.

Mime
To act out a scene or situation without using any words. The story is related to the audience by means of facial expression, gesture, and body movement.

Minimalism
"Less is more." The poem is reduced to its basic, most direct expression. No unnecessary words or images clutter the picture. See "Winter Morning" by Irene Cox.

Monologue
The poet creates a character; the poem is the character's "speech" to the reader. See "Bothering Me at Last" by David Ignatow.

Mood
Mood is the emotional environment, or atmosphere, created by the poet. A good poet can create a mood with a few words:
"Silhouettes, they lean against a ringed moon,
their heads down against the threat of snow."

R. A. Kawilikak

Muses
In literature, "muses" or "muse" refers to poetic inspiration. The Muses were Greek goddesses who presided over poetry, music, dance, and the arts.

Narrative
The story-line of the poem. A narrative poem is a poem written to tell a particular story. Many poems have very little or no narrative.

Nick
Many poems have a "nick," a particular word, phrase, line, or

stanza that grabs the reader's eye and imagination, and charges the rest of the poem with meaning.

Nonsense Verse

Verse that uses ridiculous rhymes to describe silly topics. See Ogden Nash's poems.

Onomatopoeia

The sound of the word mimics the sound to which it refers: "thud," "crackle," "buzz," and "chickadee" are onomatopoeic.

Oxymoron

(Greek: oxy = sharp, moros = dull) An expression that combines contradictory or opposite ideas, e.g., "a living death."

Paradox

An apparently contradictory statement, with an element of truth in it, e.g., the title of Paul Simon's song "The Sound of Silence."

Parody

A comic imitation of a serious poem.

Pathetic Fallacy

An artistic device. Nature reflects the feelings of the characters and the mood of the events in the story. See Red Lane's "Margins XIV."

Persona

One of the most important literary concepts. The persona who narrates, or speaks, the poem is not the living person who wrote the poem. In writing the poem, the poet always creates a persona, a speaker who is other than himself or herself. Sometimes the two resemble one another and the reader can make a connection between them. More often, the poet is assuming a role to express a special point of view.

Personification

To attribute to inanimate objects, animals, or abstract ideas the characteristics and qualities of persons.
"The hillside blushed, soaked in our broken wave."
Seamus Heaney

Petrarchan sonnet

A sonnet that is divided into an *octave* (the first eight lines) and a *sestet* (the last six lines). See also Sonnet.

Poetic Justice

Justice as one wishes it to be. The good are rewarded and the evil are punished.

Poetics

The portion of literary criticism concerned with poetry.

Point of View

The way in which something is presented, viewed, or considered. The poet's mental attitude. The tone the poet adopts in presenting the material.

Pun

A play on words; words identical or similar in sound but different in meaning. The last word of this quotation has a double meaning: "the clever/armchair so recently recovered" Carol Shields

Quatrain

A stanza of four lines. Quatrains are the most familiar of English verse forms.

Reader

"I write half the poem. The reader writes the other half." Paul Valéry

Realism

The artist chooses to present life as it actually is, without exaggeration or embellishment.

Refrain

Lines of poetry that are repeated at regular intervals within the poem. A refrain sometimes consists of a single line or even a single word. See also **Chorus**.

Rhyme

A combining agent that glues the lines of the poem together by similarity of sounds. Rhyme depends on sound not on spelling: crime/rhyme/slime/time.

Rhythm

The flow of the words and the lines of the poem. The recurrent beat or stress of the line. When the rhythm of a poem is regular, it is called metre.

Satire

A work of literature exposing the follies and weaknesses of a person or institution. Satire endeavours to bring about reform by ridiculing human frailties and customs. See Leona Gom's "Nazis."

Simile

A comparison between two things of unlike nature usually introduced by like, as, or than.
"A poem should be wordless
As the flight of birds"
                              Archibald Macleish

Shape Poetry

See **Calligram**.

Slice-of-life

An anecdotal sketch of life just as it is without adornment or enlargement.

Song

A poem written to be sung.

Sonnet

A poem with fourteen lines, with five poetic feet per line. There are different kinds of sonnets, each kind having a particular rhyme scheme and structuring of lines.

Spondee

(/ /) (héartbréak) A poetic foot. A spondee consists of two accented syllables together.

Stanza
The pattern of lines that makes up a unit of the poem. The most common stanza is the quatrain (units of four lines).

Stream of Consciousness
See **Interior Monologue**.

Structure
The way the poem is put together. See **Form**.

Symbol
Something that suggests or stands for something else.

Symbolism
Poems are suggestive. They reach beyond themselves. For example, when a poem refers to the spring season, the reader is reminded of many associated experiences and images: the renewal of vegetation, the happiness that seems to come with the season, the cycle of life, the idea of an afterlife. Each poem has its own symbolism.

Tercet
A three-line stanza.

Theme
The meaning, the point, the gist, the essence of a piece of literature.

Title
Never take a poem's title for granted. A poet often uses the title to add an extra layer of meaning or an ironic reversal. See "God Bless General Motors Whoever He Is" by Al Pittman.

Tone
The artist's attitude towards the subject of his or her poem and towards the audience. Tone ≠ mood. A poem might have a gothic mood but a satiric tone. Tone can be difficult to assess; the reader must guess the storyteller's voice and intent.

Triple Rhyme
Three syllables similar in sound: million/vermilion.

Trochee
($/\cup$) (spirit) A poetic foot. A troche consists of two syllables with the accent or stress on the first syllable.

Verse
The word "verse" generally means "stanza." It is also used to signify poetry that does not have a serious intent—e.g., light verse.

Video
(Latin = I see) Video refers to the picture portion of a film or television broadcast—or a poem. How does the poem make a picture?

This index does not include poems with anonymous authors, nor does it include poems that were written by students. For poems by students, see "Student Voices", page 228. For a complete index, see "Index of Titles", page 229.

• • **in order of appearance**

Permission to reprint copyrighted material is gratefully acknowledged. The publishers have made every effort to trace the source of materials appearing in this book. Information that will enable the publishers to rectify any error or omission will be welcomed.

MILTON ACORN "In Addition" "Charlottetown Harbour" from *Dig Up My Heart* by Milton Acorn. Used by permission of the Canadian Publishers, McClelland and Stewart, Toronto.

LILIAN ALLEN "Unnatural Causes" reprinted by permission of Verse to Vinyl.

MAYA ANGELOU "When I Think about Myself" from *Just Give Me a Cool Drink of Water 'For I Diiie* by Maya Angelou. Copyright © 1971 by Maya Angelou. Reprinted by permission of HIRT Music.

MARGARET ATWOOD "Dream 1: The Bush Garden" from *The Journals of Susanna Moodie* by Margaret Atwood. Copyright © Oxford University Press Canada 1970. "Night Poem" from *Selected Poems II: Poems Selected & New 1976-1986* by Margaret Atwood. Copyright © Margaret Atwood 1986. Reprinted by permission of Oxford University Press Canada.

WYSTAN HUGH AUDEN "The Unknown Citizen" "The Average" from *Collected Poems* by W.H. Auden. Reprinted by permission of Faber and Faber Limited.

E. J. BARRY "Golf" reprinted by permission of the author.

BILL BISSETT "every whun at 2 o'clock" from *Selected Poems* by bill bisset. Reprinted by permission of Talon Books Ltd.

ROY BLOUNT JR. "Against Broccoli" copyright © 1976 by Roy Blount Jr. Reprinted by permission of International Creative Management.

ROO BORSON "Abundance" reprinted by permission of the author.

CHRISTIAN BOUCHARD "Life in the City" reprinted by permission of the author.

EDGARD BRAGA "poema" from *Anthology of Concretism*, edited by Eugene Wildman. Published by Swallow Press Inc., Chicago: 1969. Reprinted with permission.

ELIZABETH BREWSTER "Mirrors" from *Selected Poems* by Elizabeth Brewster. Reprinted by permission of Oberon Press.

ROBERT BROWNING "Incident of the French Camp" from *The Complete Poetical Works of Robert Browning*, New Edition (New York: Macmillan, 1920).

KLAUS BURKHARDT "Loch" from *Anthology of Concretism*, edited by Eugene Wildman. Published by Swallow Press Inc., Chicago: 1969. Reprinted with permission.

KATE BUSH "Wuthering Heights" by Kate Bush. © 1978 KATE BUSH MUSIC LTD. Rights for the U.S. and Canada Controlled and Administered by BEECHWOOD MUSIC CORPORATION. All Rights Reserved. International Copyright Secured. Used by Permission.

DAVID BYRNE "(Nothing But) Flowers" by David Byrne. Copyright © 1988, Index Music, Inc. (ASCAP). Reprinted by permission.

MARITES CARINO "Unspoken Hostility" originally published in *Inkslinger 1988*. Reproduced by permission of the Saskatoon Board of Education.

HARRY CHAPIN "Mr. Tanner" "Circle" copyright © 1973 by Story Songs Ltd. Reprinted by permission of Story Songs Ltd.

HELEN CHASIN "Joy Sonnet in a Random Universe" from *Coming Close and Other Poems* by Helen Chasin. Copyright ©. Reprinted by permission of Yale University Press.

SHARI CHUDY "Square Dancing" originally published in *Inkslinger 1988*. Reproduced by permission of the Saskatooon Board of Education.

IRENE COX "Winter Morning" used by permission of the author.

COUNTEE CULLEN "Incident" reprinted by permission of GRM Associated Inc., agents for the estate of Ida M. Cullen. From the book ON THESE I STAND by Countee Cullen. Copyright © 1925 by Harper & Brothers; copyright renewed 1953 by Ida M. Cullen.

E. E. CUMMINGS "next to of course god america i" is reprinted from IS 5 poems by E. E. Cummings, Edited by George James Firmage, by permission of Liveright Publishing Corporation. Copyright © 1985 by E. E. Cummings Trust. Copyright 1926 by Horace Liveright. Copyright © 1954 by E. E. Cummings. Copyright © 1985 by George James Firmage. "Spring is like a perhaps hand" and "the/ sky/ was" are reprinted form TULIPS & CHIMNEYS by E. E. Cummings, Edited by George James Firmage, by permission of Liveright Publishing Corporation. Copyright 1923, 1925 and renewed 1951, 1953 by E. E. Cummings. Copyright © 1973, 1976 by the Trustees for the E. E. Cummings Trust. Copyright © 1973, 1976 by George James Firmage.

JAMES DALE "Drunk Driver in Concrete" reprinted by permission of the author.

CHRIS DE BURGH "A Spaceman Came Travelling" Words and Music by Chris De Burgh. Copyright © 1976 Big Secret Music Ltd. All rights in the U.S. and Canada administered by Chrysalis Music (ASCAP). International copyright secured. All rights reserved. Used by permission.

PAUL DE VREE "London" from *Speaking Pictures*, edited by Milton Klonsky and published by Crown Publishers Inc.

EMILY DICKINSON "I'm Nobody!" "I never saw a moor" reprinted by permission of the publishers and the Trustees of Amherst College from *The Poems of Emily Dickinson*, Thomas H. Johnson, ed., Cambridge, Mass.: the Belknap Press of Harvard University Press, Copyright 1951, © 1955, 1979, 1983 by the President and Fellows of Harvard College. Also from *The Complete Poems of Emily Dickinson*, edited by Thomas H. Johnson, Copyright © 1929 by Martha Dickinson Bianchi, Copyright © 1957, 1960 by Mary L. Hampson. Reprinted by permission of Little, Brown and Company.

PAUL DONEGAN "The Soaring Sixties" reprinted by permission of the author.

DON DOMANSKI "Flea" from *The Cape Breton of the Dead* by Don Domanski. Originally published by House of Anansi Press. Reprinted by permission of Stoddart Publishing Co. Limited, 34 Lesmill Rd., Don Mills, Ontario, Canada.

DAVID DUCLOS "Lionel" reprinted by permission of the author.

CASEY ELDER "Jazz" originally published in *Inkslinger 1986*. Reproduced by permission of the Saskatoon Board of Education.

MARI EVANS "The Rebel" from *I Am a Black Woman*, published by Wm. Morrow & Co., 1970. Reprinted by permission of the author.

ROBERT FRANCIS "The Base Stealer" copyright © 1948 by Robert Francis. Reprinted from *The Orb Weaver* by permission of Wesleyan University Press.

ROBERT FROST "The Death of the Hired Man" "The Road Not Taken" "Provide, Provide!" "Nothing Gold Can Stay" "The Runaway" from *The Poetry of Robert Frost* edited by Edward Connery Lathem. Copyright © 1916, 1923, 1930, 1939, 1969 by Holt, Rinehart and Winston, Inc. Copyright © 1936, 1944, 1951, 1958 by Robert Frost. Copyright © 1964, 1967 by Lesley Frost Ballantine. Reprinted by arrangement with Henry Holt and Company, Inc.

TOMIYASU FUSEI "Like a father" "I read a book—" from *Modern Japanese Haiku* edited by Makoto Ueda. Reprinted by permission of University of Toronto Press.

SHARON GAZELEY "Sunday" reprinted by permission of the author.

WILFRID WILSON GIBSON "Flannan Isle" from *Collected Poems* by W. W. Gibson. Reprinted by permission of Mr. Michael Gibson and Macmillan Company, London and Basingstoke.

JACQUES GODBOUT "Enfant" translated from the French by John Robert Colombo. Copyright © Jacques Godbout and John Robert Colombo. Originally published by Oxford University Press. Reprinted by permission.

LEONA GOM "Nazis" reprinted by permission of the author. "Late Night News" from *The Singletree* by Leona Gom. Reprinted by permission of Sono Nis Press, Victoria.

EUGEN GOMRINGER "ping pong" reprinted by permission of the author.

MICHAEL GOSSIER "the little purple man" reprinted by permission of the author.

PHYLLIS GOTLIEB *from* "This One's on Me" reprinted by permission of the author.

JOSE LINO GRUNEWALD "bois dois" from *Anthology of Concretism*, edited by Eugene Wildman. Published by Swallow Press Inc., Chicago: 1969. Reprinted with permission.

NICOLAS GUILLEN "Proposition" from *The Poetry of the Negro* edited by Langston Hughes and Arna Bontemps. Copyright © 1948 by Langston Hughes and Ben Carruthers. Copyright renewed 1976 by George Houston Bass. Reprinted by permission of Harold Ober Associates Incorporated.

GWEN HAUSER "help i've just been run over by a bus" reprinted by permission of the author.

SEAMUS HEANEY "Requiem for the Croppies" from *Door Into the Dark* by Seamus Heaney. "Changes" from *Station Island* by Seamus Heaney. "Follower" "Saint Francis and the Birds" from *Death of a Naturalist* by Seamus Heaney. Reprinted by permission of Faber and Faber Limited.

LANGSTON HUGHES "Dreams" from *The Dream Keeper and Other Poems* by Langston Hughes. Copyright © 1932 by Alfred A. Knopf, Inc. and renewed 1960 by Langston Hughes. "Dream

Variations" from *Selected Poems of Langston Hughes*. Copyright © 1926 by Alfred A. Knopf, Inc. and renewed 1954 by Langston Hughes. Reprinted by permission of Alfred A. Knopf, Inc.

DAVID IGNATOW "Bothering Me at Last" copyright © 1955 by David Ignatow. Reprinted from *Figures of the Human* by permission of Wesleyan University Press.

"INDIAN CONCEPTS" from *Red On White* by Duke Redbird and Marty Dunn. Reprinted by permission of Stoddart Publishing Co. Limited, 34 Lesmill Road, Don Mills, Ontario, Canada.

SEAN JARA "North American Nutrition" reprinted by permission of the author.

PAT JASPER "Long Way Home" from *Recycling* by Pat Jasper (Fiddlehead Poetry Books & Goose Lane Editions, 1985). Reprinted by permission of Goose Lane Editions, Fredericton, New Brunswick.

PAULETTE JILES "Paper Matches" from *Celestial Navigation* by Paulette Jiles. Used by permission of the Canadian Publishers, McClelland and Stewart, Toronto.

GEORGE JOHNSTON "War on the Periphery" reprinted by permission. Copyright © 1951, 1979 The New Yorker Magazine, Inc.

D. G. JONES "Heavens" "Field Notes" "Orchard" from *A Throw of Particles* D. G. Jones. Reprinted by permission of Stoddart Publishing Co. Limited, 34 Lesmill Rd., Don Mills, Ontario, Canada. "The Wind Disturbs" from *The Sun Is Axeman* by D. G. Jones. Reprinted by permission of the author.

TANYA KANIGAN "Thursday Night" originally published in *Inkslinger 1987*. Reproduced by permission of the Saskatoon Board of Education.

JOY KOGAWA "What Do I Remember of the Evacuation?" reprinted by permission of the author. "Day of the Bride" from *A Choice of Dreams* by Joy Kogawa. Used by permission of the Canadian Publishers, McClelland and Stewart, Toronto.

RICHARD KOSTELANETZ "DIE" "LIVE" reprinted by permission of the author.

HERBERT KRETZMER excerpts from "Red and Black" and "I Dreamed a Dream" from "LES MISERABLES." Lyrics by Herbert Kretzmer, original text by Alain Boublil and Jean-Marc Natel, music by Claude-Michel Schönberg. Music and Lyrics copyright © 1980 by Editions Musicales Alain Boublil. English Lyrics copyright © 1986 by Alain Boublil Music Ltd. Mechanical and Publication Rights for the USA Administered by Alain Boublil Music Ltd., c/o Laventhol and Horwath, 605 Third Avenue, New York, NY 10158, Tel. 212-297-4500, Telex 640279. Internaional Copyright Secured. All Rights Reserved.

TAKAHAMA KYOSHI "A butterfly" from *Modern Japanese Haiku* edited by Makoto Ueda. Reprinted by permission of University of Toronto Press.

RED LANE "Margins XIV" reprinted by permission of the author's Estate.

D.H. LAWRENCE "Piano" from *The Complete Poems of D. H. Lawrence*. © 1964, 1971 by Angelo Ravagli and C. M. Weekley, Executors of the Estate of Freida Lawrence Ravagli. Reprinted by permission of Viking Penguin, a division of Penguin Books USA Inc.

IRVING LAYTON "The Bull Calf" from *Collected Poems* by Irving Layton. Used by permission of the Canadian Publishers, McClelland and Stewart, Toronto.

RICHARD LEES "Poetry" originally published in *Inkslinger 1988*. Reproduced by permission of the Saskatoon Board of Education.

BEKLEEN LEONG "My Grandmother—The Bluebottle" from *Blackwomentalk Poetry*. Reprinted by permission of the author.

DENISE LEVERTOV."The Singer" from *Poems 1968-1972* by Denise Levertov. Copyright © 1969 by Denise Levertov Goodman. "The Secret" from *Poems 1960-1967* by Denise Levertov. Copyright © 1964 by Denise Levertov Goodman. Reprinted by permission of New Directions Publishing Corporation. Canadian rights.

GORDON LIGHTFOOT "Sit Down Young Stranger" copyright © 1969 Early Morning Music, by Gordon Lightfoot. Used by permission.

PAT LOWTHER "Rumours of War" from *A Stone Diary* by Pat Lowther. Copyright © Oxford University Press Canada 1977. Reprinted by permission of Oxford University Press Canada.

GWENDOLYN MACEWAN "The Grand Dance" from *Afterworlds* by Gwendolyn MacEwan. Used by permission of the Canadian Publishers, McClelland and Stewart, Toronto.

ARCHIBALD MACLEISH "Ars Poetica" from *New and Collected Poems 1917-1976* by Archibald MacLeish. Copyright © 1976 by Archibald MacLeish. Reprinted by permission of Houghton Mifflin Company.

RITA MACNEIL "Working Man" "Realized Your Dreams" reprinted by permission of Brookes Diamond Productions, Halifax.

ANNE MALCOLM "Untitled" originally published in *Inkslinger 1986*. Reproduced by permission of the Saskatoon Board of Education.

MARYA MANNES "Highest Standard of Living Yet" from *Subverse*. Copyright © 1959 by Marya Mannes and Robert Osborn. Reprinted by permission of George Braziller, Inc.

DON MARQUIS "the lesson of the moth" from *archy and mehitabel* by Don Marquis, copyright 1927 by Doubleday, a division of Bantam, Doubleday, Dell Publishing Group, Inc. Used by permission of the publisher.

JOHN MASEFIELD "Cargoes" "Sea-Fever" reprinted by permission of The Society of Authors as the literary representative of the Estate of John Masefield.

PHYLLIS MCGINLEY "First Lesson" from *Times Three* by Phyllis McGinley. Copyright © 1959 by Phyllis McGinley. Reprinted by permission of Viking Penguin, a division of Penguin Books USA Inc.

DON MCLEAN "Vincent (Starry, Starry Night)" Words and Music by Don McLean. Copyright © 1971, 1972 by Music Corporation of America, Inc. and Benny Bird Music. Rights administered by MCA Music Publishing, A Division of MCA Inc., New York, NY 10019. All rights reserved. Used by permission.

ALICE MEYNELL "Maternity" from *The Poems of Alice Meynell* (Oxford: Oxford University Press, 1940).

BILL MIDDLETON "Family" reprinted by permission of the author.

EDNA ST. VINCENT MILLAY "Afternoon on a Hill" by Edna St. Vincent Millay. From *Collected Poems*, Harper & Row. Copyright 1917, 1945 by Edna St. Vincent Millay. Reprinted by permission of Elizabeth Barnett, Literary Executor.

EDWIN MORGAN "The Computer's First Birthday Card" from *Poems of Thirty Years*, copyright © 1982, by Edwin Morgan. Reprinted by permission of Carcanet Press Limited.

DAVE MORICE "The Eagle" from *Poetry Comics* by Dave Morice. Reprinted by permission of Simon & Schuster, Inc.

SUSAN MUSGRAVE "What being a Strawberry means" from *Selected Strawberries and Other Poems* by Susan Musgrave. Reprinted by permission of Sono Nis Press, Victoria, B.C.

SHEIN NANJI "Hugging" by Shein Nanji (Harbord Collegiate Institute). From *Writing/Ecrits '89*, published by the Language Study Centre, Toronto Board of Education.

OGDEN NASH "The Eel" "The Panther" from *Verses From 1929 On* by Ogden Nash. Copyright © 1940, 1942, 1947, by Ogden Nash. "The Eel" first appeared in *The New Yorker*. Reprinted by permission of Little, Brown and Company.

BP NICHOL "arrow" from *As Elected* by bp Nichol, © bp Nichol, Talon Books Ltd., Vancouver 1980. "Turnips are" from *love: a book of remembrances* by bp Nichol, copyright © 1974, Talon Books Ltd. Reprinted by permission of the publisher.

SEIICHI NIIKUNI "stream bank" from *Anthology of Concretism*, edited by Eugene Wildman. Published by Swallow Press Inc., Chicago: 1969. Reprinted with permission.

KEN NORRIS "You are reading this too fast" reprinted by permission of the author.

ALDEN NOWLAN "He Sits Down on the Floor of a School for the Retarded" "Saturday Night" "An Exchange of Gifts" "Greatness" from *An Exchange of Gifts* by Alden Nowlan. "Warren Pryor" from *The Mysterious Naked Man* by Alden Nowlan. Originally published by Irwin Publishing. Reprinted by permission of Stoddart Publishing Co. Limited, 34 Lesmill Rd., Don Mills, Ontario, Canada. "In the Garden" reprinted by permission of Stoddart Publishing Co. Limited.

ALFRED NOYES "The Highwayman" from *Collected Poems* by Alfred Noyes. Reprinted by permission of John Murray (Publishers) Ltd.

MICHAEL ONDAATJE "Griffin of the Night" from *There's a Trick with a Knife I'm Learning to Do: Poems '63-'78*. Used by permission of the Canadian Publishers, McClelland and Stewart, Toronto.

WILFRED OWEN "Disabled" from *Collected Poems* by Wilfred Owen. Thanks to the Estate of Wilfred Owen and The Hogarth Press.

P. K. PAGE "The New Bicycle" reprinted by permission of the author.

SYLVIA PARKER "Motherlove" reprinted by permission of the author.

AL PITTMAN "Funeral" "God Bless General Motors Whoever He Is" from *Once When I Was Drowning* by Al Pittman. Copyright © Al Pittman. "Cooks Brook" copyright © Al Pittman. Permission for use of this material granted by Breakwater Books Ltd., St. John's, Newfoundland.

HELEN PORTER "Edith" "The Dancer" from *From This Place* (Jaesperson Press, 1977). Reprinted by permission of the author.

EDWIN JOHN PRATT "Erosion" "The Shark" from *E.J. Pratt: Complete Poems Vol 1 & 2* edited by Sandra Djwa and R.G. Moyles. Reprinted by permission of University of Toronto Press.

AL PURDY "About Being a Member of Our Armed Forces" from *Collected Poems* by Al Purdy. "Mice in the House" from *Caribou Horses* by Al Purdy. Used by permission of the Canadian Publishers, McClelland and Stewart, Toronto.

DUDLEY RANDALL "Ballad of Birmingham" reprinted by permission of Broadside Press, Detroit, Michigan.

RYAN REBELLO "Tranquil Nights" reprinted by permission of the author.

EMILE VICTOR RIEU "Sir Smasham Uppe" from *The Flattered Flying Fish: Collected Poems of E. V. Rieu*. Published by Methuen, London: 1962. Reprinted with permission.

EDWIN ARLINGTON ROBINSON "Richard Cory" from *The Children of the Night* by Edwin Arlington Robinson (New York: Scribner's, 1897).

EDWIN MEADE ROBINSON "How He Turned Out" from *Piping and Panning* by Edwin Meade Robinson, copyright © 1920, by Harcourt Brace Jovanovich, Inc., reprinted by permission of the publisher.

THEODORE ROETHKE "The Bat" from *The Collected Poems of Theodore Roethke*. Copyright © 1938 by Theodore Roethke. Used by permission of Doubleday, a division of Bantam, Doubleday, Dell Publishing Group, Inc.

JOE ROSENBLATT "Waiter! there's an alligator in my coffee" from *Bumblebee Dithyramb* by Joe Rosenblatt. Reprinted by permission of Press Porcepic.

CHRISTINA ROSSETTI "Uphill" "Who Has Seen the Wind?" from *Poetical Works* by Christina Rossetti (New York: Macmillan, 1924).

CARL SANDBURG "Chicago" from *Chicago Poems* by Carl Sandburg, copyright © 1916 by Holt, Rinehart and Winston, Inc. and renewed 1944 by Carl Sandburg, reprinted by permission of Harcourt Brace Jovanovich, Inc.

SIEGFRIED SASSOON "Dreamers" reprinted by permission of George T. Sassoon.

DUNCAN CAMPBELL SCOTT "On the Way to the Mission" from *Poems of D.C. Scott*. Used by permission of the Canadian Publishers, McClelland and Stewart, Toronto.

ROBERT SERVICE "The Cremation of Sam McGee" from *Songs of a Sourdough: Complete Poems of Robert Service*. Reprinted by permission of the author's estate.

JOSEPH SHERMAN "First and Last" originally published in *The Atlantic Anthology*. Reprinted by permission of the author.

CAROL SHIELDS "January" "Neighbour" from *Intersect* (Ottawa: Borealis Press Limited, 1974). Reprinted by permission of the publisher.

JON SILKIN "Carved" from *Selected Poems* by Jon Silkin. Reprinted by permission of Routledge, A Division of Routledge, Chapman and Hall Ltd.

PAUL SIMON "The Sound of Silence" copyright © 1964 Paul Simon. Used by permission of the publisher.

ARTHUR JAMES MARSHALL SMITH "The Lonely Land" from *The Classic Shade* by A.J.M. Smith. Used by permission of the Canadian Publishers, McClelland and Stewart, Toronto.

MARY ELLEN SOLT "Moonshot Sonnet" originally published in *Concrete Poetry*. Reprinted by permission of Indiana University Press.

RICHARD SOMMER "The Word Game" reprinted by permission of the author.

RAYMOND SOUSTER "The Launching" "The Top Hat" "The Attack" from *Collected Poems of Raymond Souster*. Reprinted by permission of Oberon Press.

BRUCE SPRINGSTEEN "My Hometown" © Bruce Springsteen. ASCAP. Reprinted by permission of the author and his agent.

DAWN TWEEDIE "True Love" originally published in *Inkslinger 1986*. Reproduced by permission of the Saskatoon Board of Education.

IAN TYSON "Four Strong Winds" (Ian Tyson) Copyright © 1963 WARNER BROS. INC. All Rights Reserved. Used By Permission.

TIMM UHLRICHS "rose" "reden" from *Anthology of Concretism*, edited by Eugene Wildman. Published by Swallow Press Inc., Chicago: 1969. Reprinted with permission.

LOUIS UNTERMEYER "Caliban in the Coal Mines" reprinted by permission of Norma A. Untermeyer & Laurence S. Untermeyer.

FRANS VANDERLINDE "ELIMINATION" from *Anthology of Concretism*, edited by Eugene Wildman. Published by Swallow Press Inc., Chicago: 1969. Reprinted with permission.

ALICE VANWART "Photographs" from *Stories to Finish* by Alice VanWart. Reprinted by permission of Sono Nis Press, Victoria, B.C. "From the Inside Out" from *Positionings* by Alice VanWart. Reprinted by permission of the author.

FRED WAH "my father hurt—" from *Breathin' My Name with a Sigh* by Fred Wah, copyright © 1974, Talon Books Ltd. Reprinted by permission of the publisher.

TOM WAYMAN "Unemployment" reprinted by permission of the author.

ACKNOWLEDGMENTS

JACOB WICKLAND "Please Do Not Feed the Seals" originally published in *Inkslinger 1988*. Reproduced by permission of the Saskatoon Board of Education.

EMMETT WILLIAMS "like attracts like" from *Selected Shorter Poems 1950-70* by Emmett Williams.

RUTH WILSON "Strike" originally published in *Waves* (Spring 1986). Reprinted with permission of the author.

HUMBERT WOLFE "The Grey Squirrel" from *Kensington Gardens* by Humbert Wolfe. Reprinted by permission of A&C Black (Publishers) Limited.

JIM WONG-CHU "equal opportunity" from *Chinatown Ghosts* by Jim Wong-Chu. Copyright © 1986. Reprinted by permission of Pulp Press, A Division of Arsenal Pulp Press Ltd., Vancouver.

JUDITH WRIGHT "Legend" "Birds" reproduced from *The Gateway* by kind permission of the publishers, Angus & Robertson (UK).

ELINOR WYLIE "Sea Lullaby" copyright © 1921 by Alfred A. Knopf, Inc. & renewed 1949 by William Rose Benet. Reprinted from *Collected Poems* by Elinor Wylie, by permission of the publisher.

DALE ZIEROTH "120 Miles North of Winnipeg" from *Clearing: Poems from a Journey* by Dale Zieroth (Toronto: House of Anansi Press, 1973). Reprinted by permission of Stoddart Publishing Co. Limited, 34 Lesmill Rd., Don Mills, Ontario, Canada.